SOUTHERN WRITERS

BIOGRAPHICAL AND CRITICAL STUDIES

BY
WILLIAM MALONE BASKERVILL

VOLUME I

GORDIAN PRESS
NEW YORK
1970

First Published 1897
Reprinted 1970

PS
261
B32
Vol. 1

61064

Published by GORDIAN PRESS, INC.
Library of Congress Catalog Card Number-70-93242
SBN   87752-005-4

Preface.

———

Since 1870 Southern writers have been conspicuous contributors to the nation's literature, rendering it both more widely national and more representatively American. The time has not yet arrived for attempting to place a final estimate upon any portion of this contribution; but a presentation of the conditions under which these writers have labored and a narrative of some of the personal facts which have influenced their writings will tend, it is hoped, to stimulate a desire for a more intimate acquaintance with this literature, which is so fresh, original, and racy of the soil. The earlier writers of this period attracted unusual attention, and most readers beyond forty may recall the rapture of glad surprise with which each new Southern writer was hailed, as he or she revealed negro, mountaineer, cracker, or creole life and character to the world. There was joy in beholding the roses of romance and poetry blossoming above the ashes of defeat and humiliation, and that too among a people hitherto more re-

markable for the masterful deeds of warrior and statesmen than for the finer,
rarer, and more artistic creations of literary genius. To this was added the ex-
hilaration of fresh and novel discoveries,
of making the acquaintance of new re-
gions and new peoples. Whether the
discoverers reported mere transcriptions
from contemporary life and manners or
threw over scenery, incident, situation,
and character the unfading light of idealizing and creative imagination—all were
gladly welcomed. But that day quickly
passed, and there is nothing novel now
either in Southern authorship or Southern topics and scenes. We have long
since grown familiar with both. Under
these more natural conditions we can
therefore the more easily take note of that
which has already been accomplished.

At first it was thought that a tolerably
complete survey of this literary movement
which so rapidly spread over the entire
South could be made in a series of twelve
short papers. But the increasing interest
in the study of Lanier's poetry, as well as
the intrinsic worth of the man and his
message, carried this paper far beyond
the limits originally intended. Further
consideration of the subject has also
induced me to include among the num-

Preface.

ber of typical writers "Sherwood Bonner," the first Southern writer to use negro character with artistic effect in literature, and Madison Cawein and Mrs. Burton Harrison, two of the most promising of our more recent writers, so that the revised list will embrace Irwin Russell, Joel Chandler Harris, Maurice Thompson, Sidney Lanier, George W. Cable, "Charles Egbert Craddock," James Lane Allen, Thomas Nelson Page, Richard Malcolm Johnston, Mrs. Burton Harrison, Miss Grace King, "Sherwood Bonner," Mrs. Margaret J. Preston, Samuel Minturn Peck, and Madison Cawein. In a closing chapter the works of various other Southern writers of fiction at the present time will be discussed.

This pioneer attempt to survey the entire field of this unique post-bellum literature, to indicate its inherent unity, and to work out some of the details characteristic of its production and of the product itself is, I trust, the not too ambitious aim of this series of papers which it is hoped may tend to secure in the nation at large a just estimate of the South's latest contribution to the common storehouse of American literature.

W. M. BASKERVILL.

VANDERBILT UNIVERSITY, *August* 26, 1897.

v

Contents.

(vii)

Irwin Russell.

A YOUNG Marylander, a stripling just from college, was dreaming dreams from which he was awakened by the guns of Sumter. One sleepless night in April, 1861, he wrote the poem, " My Maryland," which may not inaptly be called the first note of the new Southern literature—" new in strength, new in depth, new in the largest elements of beauty and truth." He that had ears to hear might have heard in the booming of those guns not only the signal for a gigantic contest, but also the proclamation of the passing away of the old order, and along with it the waxflowery, amateurish, and sentimental race of Southern writers.

But first should come the terrible experiences of a mighty conflict, in which the soul of the people was to be brought out through struggles, passions, partings, heroism, love, death—all effective in the production of genuine feeling and the development of real character. While the battles were being fought in the homes of the Southerners, their poets sent forth, now a stirring, martial lyric, now a humorous song or poem recounting the trials and hardships of camp, hospital, and prison life, these becoming ever more and more intermingled with dirges—for Jackson, for Albert Sidney Johnston, for Stuart, for Ashby, and finally for the " Conquered Banner." But in all of these there was no trace of artificiality, no sign of mawkish sentimentality. They were surcharged with deep, genuine, sincere feeling; they were instinct with life. In this respect the war poetry laid the foundation for the new literature.

Accompanying the return to reality was a social earthquake which laid bare the rich literary deposits in

which the South abounded. As one
of the best of the new school has
said, "Never in the history of this
country has there been a generation
of writers who came into such an
inheritance of material as has fallen
to these younger writers of the
South." Under the new order
Southern life and manners were for
the first time open to a full and free
report and criticism.

It is noticeable that in the racy,
humorous writings of Longstreet,
Thompson, Meek, a n d others—
sketches which contained the elements of real life—the negro is conspicuous for his absence. At that
time there was enough and to spare
written about him by way of defense,
vindication, or apology, but to use
him as art material seemed to be far
from the thoughts of Southern writers. The only notable book in which
negro character was made use of
chanced to be a phenomenal success ;
but as it was written on the principle

of antagonism, and as it really served
as the signal for the deadly struggle
which followed, it was altogether
natural that Southern writers would
not imitate this example. After the
war, however, the one subject which
hitherto could have been treated with
least freedom became the most prolific theme of the new writers. Consciously or unconsciously, they one
and all, with one noteworthy exception, adopted a method diametrically
opposed to that of the author of
" Uncle Tom's Cabin." They were
either those whose lives had been
purified in the fires of adversity and
defeat, or buoyant, ardent young
souls "with the freshness of early
dew upon their wings."

This literature of the new South
had for its cardinal principles good
will and sympathy. Its aims were
to cement bonds of good fellowship
between the sections, to depict the
negro according to his real character,
and to exhibit to the world the true

4

relations which existed between master and slave.

Irwin Russell was among the first, if not the very first, of Southern writers to appreciate the literary possibilities of the negro character and of the unique relations existing between the two races before the war, and was among the first to develop them, says Joel Chandler Harris. This skillful delineator of unique and peculiar character was naturally drawn to the sensitive, erratic, but exquisitely attuned young poet, and he contributed the "Introduction" when his slender remnant was published in 1888 by the Century Company under the title: "Poems by Irwin Russell." The whole story is told in a few simple words by Mr. Harris, in which he says of Russell: "He possessed in a remarkable degree what has been described as the poetical temperament, and though he was little more than twenty-six years old at the time of his death, his sufferings and his sorrows made his life a long one. He had at his command everything that affection could suggest; he had loyal friends wherever he went; but in spite of all this, the waywardness of genius led continually in the direction of suffering and sorrow. In the rush and hurly-burly of the practical, everyday world he found himself helpless; and so, after a brief struggle, he died."

It is surprising how few in the South know anything of this young poet except his name, and many have never heard that. Only one sketch of him has found its way into the literary journals, and that is a very interesting and valuable paper in the *Critic*, written by Charles C. Marble, who seems to have had a close personal acquaintance with the "unhappy boy." Another paper of still more vividly personal interest was written by Catherine Cole and published in the *New Orleans Times-*

Irwin Russell.

Democrat. But for much of the
personal matter the writer is indebted to the young poet's mother, who,
though an invalid, is still living.

In Irwin Russell's veins mingled
the blood of Virginia and of New
England. His paternal great-grandfather was a soldier of the Revolution, and hailed from the Old Do-
minion. His grandfather was born
and reared in this state, but after
reaching manhood he went thence
to Ohio, where he settled and married a woman of fine intellect, a native of the Isle of Wight, Miss
Mary McNab. One of their sons is
still living, Mr. Addison P. Russell,
who was formerly Secretary of
State in Ohio, but is better known
now as the author of several books:
"Library Notes," "A Club of One,"
and "In a Club Corner." Irwin's
father, Dr. William McNab Russell,
grew up in Ohio, studied medicine,
and was married to a young lady, a
native of New York, but of New

7

England ancestry. The newly married pair then sought a home in Mississippi, settling at Port Gibson, where the young doctor engaged in the practice of medicine, becoming in a short time very successful. Here it was, June 3, 1853—the year in which the author of " Marse Chan" first saw the light in Virginia—that Irwin Russell was born. Almost immediately, at three months of age, he was subjected to an attack of yellow fever, which terrible scourge was then raging as an epidemic. That same year the family and home were transferred to St. Louis, Mo., where they remained until the breaking out of the Civil War. Then Dr. Russell took his family back to Port Gibson to cast in his lot with the Confederacy ; for, like almost every Northerner that had made his home in the South, he was an ardent sympathizer with this section.

While at St. Louis Irwin was

placed in school, for he was a remarkably precocious boy, having
learned to read well at four years of
age. He was a diligent little student, and so general was his information that his young friends used
to call him the "walking cyclopedia."
Again, after the war, he was sent
back to this city to be placed in the
St. Louis University, which was
under the charge of the Jesuit fathers, and from which he was graduated in 1869 with high credit. At
college he kept up his studious habits and gave evidence of real ability,
his talents being more particularly
shown in the line of higher mathematics. Mr. Marble writes: "I remember hearing him talk brilliant-
ly of the science of navigation, of
which, theoretically, he was master.
He had discovered a method of exactly ascertaining the latitude from
observations of the sun's altitude
and deviation from the meridian;
and when it was favorably reported

upon by certain scientific persons he
immediately applied to the captain of
a ship for the privilege of making a
voyage with him, that he might test
and increase his knowledge of navigation."

After graduation he returned to
Mississippi, read law, and by a special act of the Legislature he was
admitted to the bar at the age of
nineteen. He practiced for awhile,
and became specially proficient in
conveyancing, which is said to require very exact technical knowledge. But one of his peculiar tastes
and disposition could hardly be expected to confine himself to the
daily routine and drudgery of a law
office. He was inclined to diver-
sions; one, for example, was the
printer's trade, which he learned so
thoroughly as to become a dainty
compositor, and in time he grew to
be critically fond of old prints and
black-letter volumes — a real con-
noisseur, recognizing at a glance

the various types used in book-making. He delighted to pick up odd volumes of the old dramatists, and took special pride in possessing one of the oldest copies of Wycherly in existence. He was also given to roving; and, like Robert Louis Stevenson, he might have been known and pointed out for the pattern of an idler. Once, when under the spell which Captain Marryatt not infrequently has thrown over a romantic and impulsive youth, he left home, Mr. Marble tells us, much to the discomfort of his parents, and lived in a sailors' boarding house in New Orleans. While there he habitually dressed as a sailor, and one day he applied for a position to a captain about to sail to the Mediterranean. "Abandoning for the time being," continues Mr. Marble, " his spectacles (which, as he had when he was only two years old lost the sight of one eye by the stab of a penknife which he unfortunately found lying open, and was nearsighted in the other, was a serious matter), he rowed out alongside the ship and with the greatest difficulty got on board. He was examined, of course, minutely and critically by the first mate, and told to come the next day. But he saw the probability of long and hard service, and abandoned the notion of thus seeing life, even if he could have succeeded in concealing his blindness till the ship sailed. But the sea never ceased to have " a perpetual fascination for him."

Fields for observation and for the study of character were thus offered to his inner eye, however much the outer ones were shut in by blindness and nearsightedness. The grotesque appealed to him strongly, and as he had acquired facility in drawing, he made numerous and fantastic sketches on scraps of paper, old envelopes, or whatever

was at hand, as material for future
use.   His skill in caricature remind-
ed his friends not a little of Thackeray.   Love of nature was in him a
passion ; and a splendid sunset, a
gorgeous Southern forest, or other
natural scenes, he keenly enjoyed
and beautifully described. Mr. Marble says : " He saw every bird, took
note of every strange conformation
of nature, was familiar with the
names of trees and plants, had an
eye for prospects, an ear for sound,
an exquisite sensitiveness for nature's perfume, and a rollicking enjoyment of the country." He was
also very fond of music, played the
piano well, and was an expert on
the banjo. His talents were versatile, and in him was found the exquisite delicacy of organism so frequently seen in modern poets, which
vibrated to every appeal. He was
sensitive alike to internal and external impressions, changes of weather
or temperature, grotesque or humor-

ous characters, different manners and tongues, and particularly responsive to the influences of the great masters of fiction and poetry.

At some time or other Irwin Russell must have had a rarely sympathetic companion or guide in literary study. Was it one of the Jesuit fathers, or his own father, " who was idolized by the son? " We know not. But his extreme nicety in the use of language, his quick and retentive ear for dialect, his ability to imitate almost perfectly the poets, and his deep reading in literature for one of his age were all remarkable and gave evidence of careful training and study. He was another example of that rare union of bright mind with frail body through which the keenest appreciation and the most exquisite sensibility are developed.

At times, too, he was capable of painstaking application and ardent devotion to study. He made a

14

close study of Chaucer and "Percy's Reliques," and the old English dramatists were his constant
companions, the sources of never-
failing enjoyment. He caught the
tones of Herrick or Thackeray's
ballads with equal ease; greatly
admired Byron, and was powerfully
influenced by Shelley. In his correspondence there was here an echo
of Carlyle, there of Thackeray or
some other master. Though his
reading was confined mainly to
English literature, he knew Mo-
lière's dramas, even wishing to
translate "Tartufe" and "Le Mis-
anthrope," and took the keenest delight in Rabelais, whose wit, sarcasm, and satiric exaggeration he
longed to apply to the follies and
deformities of more modern life.
"The margins of his copy of this
author," says a friend, "and many
interleaved pages were filled with
notes and comments; and William
Dove himself, whom Southey de-

scribes as a ' practical Pantagruelist,' was not more influenced by his pages. He literally, as he somewhere says, had the best parts of Rabelais by heart."

But his chief favorite was Burns, whose influences are everywhere visible. " Christmas Night in the Quarters " reminds us strongly now of the "Jolly Beggars," now of " Tam O'Shanter." His imitation of Burns's " Epistles " is so perfect that we could easily believe that the Scottish bard wrote the following stanzas :

> The warld, they say, is gettin' auld;
> Yet in her bosom, I've been tauld,
> A burnin', youthfu' heart's installed—
>   I dinna ken—
> But sure her face seems freezin' cauld
>   To some puir men.
>
> In summer, though the sun may shine,
> Aye still the winter's cauld is mine·
> But what o' that? The manly pine
>   Endures the storm!
> Ae spark o' Poesy divine
>   Will keep me warm.

Irwin Russell.

In almost boyish abandon he
says: "Burns is my idol. He
seems to me the greatest man that
ever God created, beside whom all
other poets are utterly insignificant.
In fact, my feelings in this regard
are precisely equivalent to those of
the old Scotchman mentioned in 'Library Notes,' who was consoled in
the hour of death by the thought
that he should see Burns."

For the writing of negro dialect
and the delineation of negro character Irwin Russell had the gift of
genius and all the advantages of
opportunity. As he himself said:
"I have lived long among the
negroes (as also long enough away
from them to appreciate their peculiarities); understand their character, disposition, language, customs,
and habits; have studied them, and
have them continually before me."
But with him dialect was a second
consideration. He used it as
Shakespeare did in "King Lear,"

17

as Fielding did in "Joseph An-
drews," as Scott, Thackeray,
George Eliot, and all the great
masters have used it—as the only
natural medium for the presentation of certain kinds of character.
In another garb they would be mas-
querading. As the author of "Uncle Remus" has aptly said, "The
dialect is not always the best—it is
often carelessly written—but the
negro is there, the old-fashioned,
unadulterated negro, who is still
dear to the Southern heart. There
is no straining after effect—indeed,
the poems produce their result by
indirection; but I do not know
where could be found to-day a hap-
pier or a more perfect representation of negro character."

Not the least important of the
shaping influences which contributed to this result is sympathetically
suggested by "One Mourner," in
"Befo' de War," "Whar's sorry
Marse Irwin's dead:"

Irwin Russell.

He couldn' 'a' talked so nachal
   'Bout niggers in sorrow and joy,
Widdouten he had a black mammy
   To sing to him 'long ez a boy.

But his chief title to our consideration is originality. As Mr. Page has said, "He laid bare a lead in which others have since discovered further treasures." Like many another original discovery, this was made in a very simple, natural way. To a friend who asked him how he came to write in negro dialect, he answered: "It was almost an inspiration. I did not reduce the trifle to writing until some time afterwards, and then, from want of recollection, in a much condensed and emasculated form. You know that I am something of a banjoist. Well, one evening I was sitting in our back yard in old Mississippi, 'twanging' on the banjo, when I heard the missis—our colored domestic, an old darky of the Aunt Dinah pattern—singing one of the

19

Irwin Russell.

outlandish camp meeting hymns of which the race is so fond. She was an extremely 'ligious character and, although seized with the impulse to do so, I hesitated to take up the tune and finish it. I did so, however, and in the dialect that I have adopted, and which I then thought, and still think, is in strict conformity to their use of it, I proceeded, as one inspired, to compose verse after verse of the most absurd, extravagant, and, to her, irreverent rhyme ever before invented, all the while accompanying it on the banjo, and imitating the fashion of the plantation negro. The old missis was so exasperated and indignant that she predicted all sorts of dire calamities. Meantime my enjoyment of it was prodigious. I was then about sixteen, and as I had soon after a like inclination to versify, was myself pleased with the performance, and it was accepted by the publisher, I have continued to work the vein indefinitely. There is much in it, such as it is."

Russell's appreciation of the darky was wonderful. The negro's humor and his wisdom were a constant marvel to him. What would strike an ordinary observer as merely ludicrous glistened by the reflected light of his mind like a proverb. The darky's insight into human nature and circumstances he believed to be more than instinct: such infallible results could only come from deduction. When asked whether there was any real poetry in the negro character, he replied: "Many think the vein a limited one, but I tell you that it is inexhaustible. The Southern negro has only just so much civilization as his contact with the white man has given him, He has only been indirectly influenced by the discoveries of science, the inventions of human ingenuity, and the general progress of mankind. Without education or social intercourse with intelligent and cultivated people, his thought has necessarily been original. . . . He has not been controlled in his convictions by historic precedent, and yet he has often manifested a foresight and wisdom in practical matters worthy of the higher races. You may call it instinct, imitation, what you will; it has, nevertheless, a foundation. I am a Democrat, was a Rebel, but I have long felt that the negro, even in his submission and servitude, was conscious of a higher nature, and must some day assert it. . . . I have felt that the soul could not be bound, and must find a way for itself to freedom. The negro race, too, in spite of oppression, has retained qualities found in few others under like circumstances. Gratitude it has always been distinguished for; hospitality and helpfulness are its natural creed; brutality, considering the prodigious depth of its degradation, is unusual. It does not lack courage, industry, self-denial, or virtue. . . . So the negro has done an immense amount of quiet thinking; and with only such forms of expression as his circumstances furnished him he indulges in paradox, hyperbole, aphorism, sententious comparison. He treasures his traditions; he is enthusiastic, patient, long-suffering, religious, reverent. Is there not poetry in the character?"

The "Poems" contain for the most part a picture of the negro himself. But only once is he in a reminiscential vein, when we catch a glimpse of the old-time prosperous planter, "Mahsr John," who "shorely wuz the greates' man de country ebber growed:"

I only has to shet my eyes, an' den it
    seems to me
I sees him right afore me now, jes like
    he use' to be,
A settin' on de gal'ry, lookin' awful big
    an' wise,

Wid little niggers fannin' him to keep
    away de flies.
He alluz wore de berry bes' ob planter's
    linen suits,
An' kep' a nigger busy jes a blackin' ob
    his boots,
De buckles on his galluses wuz made ob
    solid gol',
An di'mons! dey was in his shut as thick
    as it would hol'.

There is a slight touch of pathos in

He had to pay his debts, an' so his lan' is
    mos'ly gone,
An' I declar' I's sorry fur my pore ol'
    Mahsr John,

but it does not prevent him from
hiding " rocks " in the bale of cotton
which, in another poem, he endeav-
ors to sell to " Mahsr Johnny."

In general the poems rather give
true presentments of the negro's
queer superstitions and still queerer
ignorances; his fondness for a story,
especially an animal tale or a ghost
story; his habit of talking to himself or the animal that he is plowing
or driving; his gift in prayer and

shrewd preachments; his love of
music, especially on the fiddle and
the banjo, and the happy abandon-
ment of his revels; his irresponsible
life, his slippery shifts, his injured
innocence when discovered—over all
of which are thrown the mantle of
charity and the mellowing rays of
humor and wisdom. Occasionally
we chance upon a dainty bit of poetry, as in the verse:

An' folks don't 'spise de vi'let flower bekase it ain't de rose.

But oftener it is practical, homespun
wit, in which " Christmas Night in
the Quarters," the best delineation
of some phases of negro life yet
written, specially abounds. Now it
is old Jim talking to a slow ox:

Mus' be you think I's dead,
    An' dis de huss you's draggin';
You's mos' too lazy to draw yo' bref,
    Let 'lone drawin' de waggin.

Then Brudder Brown, with native simplicity, proceeds " to beg a
blessin' on dis dance: "

Irwin Russell.

Oh Mahsr! let dis gath'rin' fin' a blessin'
  in yo' sight!
Don't jedge us hard f·ir what we does—
  you know it's Christmus night.

.   .   .   .

You bless us, please, Sah, eben ef we's
  doin' wrong to-night ;
'Kase den we'll need de blessin' more'n
  ef we's doin' right.

The dance begins—and a more **nat**-ural scene than the fiddler " callin' de figgers " was never penned—in which " Georgy Sam " carries off the palm.

> De nigger mus' be, fur a fac',
> Own cousin to a jumpin' jack!

"An tell you what, de *supper* wuz a 'tic'lar sarcumstance," the poet himself not even attempting to describe this scene. But the fun reaches its height when the banjo is called for, and the story of its origin is told: how Ham invented it " fur to amuse hese'f " in the ark. Did Burns ever sing a more rollicking strain than this?

26

Irwin Russell.

He strung her, tuned her, struck a jig—
   'twas " Nebber Min' de Wedder "—
She soun' like forty-lebben bands a play-
   in' all togedder;
Some went to pattin', some to dancin';
   Noah called de figgers,
An' Ham he sot an' knocked de tune, de
   happiest ob niggers!

So wears the night, and wears so fast,
All wonder when they find it past,
And hear the signal sound to go
From what few cocks are left to crow.

The picture of the freedman is
strikingly characteristic and true to
life. The false sample of cotton
and the hidden stones in the bale
being detected, he is, as usual, ready
enough with an excuse:

       Mahsr Johnny, dis is fine.
I's gone and hauled my brudder's cotton
  in, instead ob mine.

He is a great flatterer and has a
" slick tongue," either in begging a
piece of tobacco or in wheedling
" young marster " out of a dollar
for a pup not " wuf de powder it'd

27

Irwin Russell.

take to blow him up." His propensity for chickens is notorious;

An' ef a man cain't borry what's layin'
    out ob nights,
I'd like you fur to tell me what's de good
    of *swivel rights?*

He thinks you "turn State's ebbydence" with a crank, and "dem folks in de Norf is de beatin'est lot!" In spite of their blue coats and brass buttons—

I seed 'em de time 'at Grant's army come
    froo—

his opinion is:

      Dey's ign'ant as ign'ant kin be.
Dey wudn't know gumbo, ef put in dey
    mouf—
Why don't dey all sell out an' come to
    de Souf?

The negro's insight, observation, and sententiousness are revealed through many homely but inimitable aphorisms:

But ef you quits a workin' ebbery time
    de sun is hot,
De sheriff's goin' to lebby upon ebbery-
    t'ing you's got.

28

Irwin Russell.

I nebber breaks a colt afore he's old
    enough to trabbel;
I nebber digs my taters tell dey's plenty
    big to grabble.
I don't keer how my apple looks, but
    on'y how it tas'es.
De man what keeps pullin' de grapevine
    shakes down a few bunches at leas'.
A violeen is like an 'ooman, mighty hard
    to guide.
.   .   .   .
Dere's alluz somefin' 'bout it out ob kel-
    ter, more or less,
An' tain't de fancies'-lookin' ones dat
    alluz does de best.
You nebber heerd a braggin' fiddler
    play a decent jig.

There is a touch of sentiment in
the father's parting precepts to his
son, about to seek his fortune as
waiter upon the " Robbut E. Lee: "

It's hard on your mudder, your leabin'—I
    don' know whatebber she'll do;
An' shorely your fader'll miss you—I'll
    alluz be thinkin' ob you.

But he quickly veils it under true
humor and homely wisdom:

Don't you nebber come back, sah, widout
    you has money an' clo'es,

29

Irwin Russell.

I's kep' you as long as I's gwine to, an'
  now you an' me we is done,
An' calves is too skace in dis country
  to kill for a prodigal son.

All these pictures are perfectly
truthful, but as the lawyers say,
they are not the whole truth. Perhaps Russell died too young to
sound the depths of the negro's
emotional nature. He caught no
tones like those echoing in Harris's
" Bless God, he died free!" or James
Whitcomb Riley's wail of the old
mother over her dead " Gladness,"
her only freeborn child.

The last two years of Russell's
life present the strange contrasts so
often met with in poetical temper-
aments when the earthborn and the
celestial have not been brought into
perfect harmony. Acts of nobility
and self-sacrifice were quickly followed by thoughtless follies which
laid him low. During the whole of
the yellow fever epidemic in 1878 he
remained in Port Gibson and served

30

as a devoted nurse, though he never escaped from the scenes through which he passed. The ghastly picture haunted his imagination. Two letters written to a friend at the time lift the curtain upon this terrible tragedy of human suffering and helplessness to which he was so nobly ministering.

September 1, 1878, he writes: "All of us are well worn out, nursing; yet we cannot nurse the sick properly, there are so many of them, and many die for want of attention. It is horrible here, you cannot conceive how horrible. Of all who have died here, not one has had any sort of funeral. Rich or poor, there is no difference. As soon as the breath leaves them they are boxed up in pine coffins and buried without the least ceremony of any kind, and nobody to follow them to the grave."

And again on the 30th: " I am worn out from nursing night and day, and performing such other duties as were mine as a ' Howard,' and simply as a man. Four days ago I, for the first time in a month, sat down to a regularly cooked and served meal. I have been living, like Dr. Wango Tango of nursery fame, ' on a biscuit a day,' when I could get it. Happily the epidemic is nearly over in town for want of material. Between six hundred and seven hundred people (out of sixteen hundred) remained in town to face the fever. Out of these there have been about five hundred and seventy cases and one hundred and eighteen deaths up to this date. I will not attempt to give you an idea of the awful horrors I have seen, among which I have lived for the past five or six weeks, besides which I have seen or heard nothing whatever. Hendrik Conscience, Boccaccio, and DeFoe tried to describe similar scenes, and I now realize how utterly they failed. No description can convey a tithe of the reality."

To crown Irwin's misfortunes, his father, whom he idolized and " who had exhausted himself in philanthropic efforts to arrest the scourge," suddenly died. Finely endowed as he was, and developing in very early life a taste for nothing so much as literature, he resisted the efforts of his family to find for him a place in a commercial or monotonous, commonplace calling. Now thrown entirely upon himself, he endeavored to take up life in a manly, courageous way, and set out with many valuable pieces in his literary knapsack for New York City, with the purpose of devoting himself to letters. Here, as everywhere, he found good friends and true, especially Mr. H. C. Bunner, Mr. R.W. Gilder, and Mr. R. U. Johnson, of *Scribner's Monthly*, and others; and the love, tenderness, and comprehending sympathy with which these men gath-

ered about the boy, trying to shield
him from his own weakness, must
have been inexpressibly sweet to
him, as it is gratefully treasured by
his mother to this day, " although I
knew," as he said to a friend with
boyish sob, " that I would win, not
they." He had exhausted all his
funds, but shrank from the thought
of again calling upon those who had
so often befriended him, when he
was taken ill of a fever. Mr. Bunner and Mr. Johnson cared for and
nursed him, and during the slow
days of his convalescence, his head
still seriously affected, he could remember nothing of the time but
" the mad wish to run away "—from
himself, which he had before attempted. So, dazed in mind, he
wandered down to the docks and
upon the decks of the " Knicker-
bocker," where he begged to be allowed to work his way to New Orleans. " Gaunt and weak and wretched as I was, they took me," said he,

telling his sad story to " Catherine
Cole," "and I did a coal heaver and
fireman's duty almost all the way
down. Landed here, I had no money, no friends, no clothes. I was
as black as an imp of Satan, and had
a very devil of despair in my heart.
I wrote out some stuff—an account
of the trip, I believe—and signing
my own name to it, took it to the
office of the *New Orleans Times*.
The city editor, Maj. Robinson,
took my copy, looked me over as if
he wondered how such a dirty
wretch ever got hold of it, and
asked me how I came by it. I told
him that I had traveled south on the
ship with Mr. Russell, and that he
had sent me. ' Go back and tell Mr.
Russell that I would be pleased to
see him,' said the Major, and I did
so. I could not present myself
again at the *Times* office, so I left a
letter there, telling the whole truth,
and winding up thus : ' What a time
I had in that den of a fireman's fore-

castle, living on tainted meat and
genuine Mark Twain "slum-gul-
lion," I won't try to tell you. I
only tell you all this to make you
understand why I did not let you
know I was my own messenger last
night. I never was in such a state
before in all my life, and was ashamed
to make myself known. However,
needs must when the devil drives.
I suppose I am not the only sufferer
from Panurge's disease, lack o'
money, but it is hard to smoke the
pipe of contentment when you can't
get tobacco.'"

From this time till he died Irwin
Russell was a semi-attaché of the
Times staff, and Mrs. Fields ("Catherine Cole"), who was in charge of
the "All Sorts" column, tells how he
came daily into her den to scratch
off a rhyme or two in inimitable
style, adding: "He was gentle and
genial, a fellow of infinite jest, and
it was no wonder he made loyal
friends wherever he went." But he

was now absolutely without hope
" I have always known it," he would
say to her, "with a sort of second
sight and a premonition of these
days, for I believe these are my
last days. I feel now, so old am I,
as if I could not remember the age
when occasionally the desire for
some unnatural stimulant did not
possess me with a fury of desire.
This has been stronger than ambition, stronger than love. I have
stretched my moral nature like a
boy playing with a piece of elastic,
knowing I should snap it presently.
. . . It has been the romance of
a weak young man threaded in
with the pure love of a mother, a
beautiful girl who hoped to be my
wife, and friends who believed in
my future. I have watched them
lose heart, lose faith, and again and
again I have been so stung and
startled that I resolved to save myself in spite of myself. . . . I
never shall."

Irwin Russell.

Only a few days after one of
these conversations this same friend
and others went with their little
wreaths of Christmas flowers down
into the heart of Franklin Street, a
wretched, noisy, dirty neighborhood, and into a forlorn little house,
set right upon the street, on whose
small wooden shutters hung a bow
with floating ends of white tarlatan
pinched out rudely at the edges.
Children, barefooted and ragged,
played in the dusty street; curious,
careless passers-by, to whom the
youth was all unknown, stopped at
the sign of the white bow, and entered in to gaze with ghoulish curiosity upon the stilled form. A
policeman stood at the head of the
casket, and near by was a faded,
sad-eyed little woman, who held out
a bundle of letters, the last he had
received from his mother and sweet-
heart. This poor Irish woman living here with her three children
rented him a rocm and cooked his

38

simple meals. He was a veritable
stranger to her. His only claim on
her was the pittance he paid for
food and lodging. But for divine
charity's sake she had watched
him through the last hours of his
sad life. Hers were the steady
arms that held him when delirium
seized him; hers were the hands
that administered medicine and food;
her time and her sympathy were
freely given; and when at midnight
he died, on a poor cot, in a poor
room up under the roof, her prayers
were the white wings of the guard-
ian angel that accompanied the departing soul through the valley of
the shadow of death.

"Ah! if we pity the good and
weak man who suffers undeserved-
ly, let us deal very gently with him
from whom misery extorts not only
tears, but shame; let us think humbly and charitably of the human nature that suffers so sadly and falls
so low. Whose turn may it be to-

morrow? What weak heart, confident before trial, may not succumb under temptation invincible? Cover the good man who has been vanquished; cover his face and pass on." His remains were first laid away in New Orleans, but subsequently removed to St. Louis, to be placed by the side of his father's, so that even the pious wish of "One Mourner" was denied him.

An' I hopes dey lay him to sleep, seh,
 Somewhar' whar' de birds will sing
About him de livelong day, seh,
 An' de flowers will bloom in spring.

But he still lives as the "Southern humorist," his pitiful story softens our hearts and his blithe spirit sweetens and refreshes our lives.

Joel Chandler Harris.

MIDDLE GEORGIA is the birthplace and home of the raciest and most original kind of Southern humor. In this quarter native material was earliest recognized and first made use of. A school of writers arose who looked out of their eyes and listened with their ears, who took frank interest in things for their own sake, and had enduring astonishment at the most common. They seized the warm and palpitating facts of everyday existence, and gave them to the world with all the accompaniments of quaint dialect, original humor, and Southern plantation life. The Middle Georgians are a simple, healthy, homogeneous folk, resembling for the most part other Southerners of like rank and calling in their manners, customs, and general

41

way of living. But they have developed a certain manly, vigorous, fearless independence of thought and action, and an ever increasing propensity to take a humorous view of life. In their earlier writings it is a homely wit, in which broad humor and loud laughter predominate; but tears are lurking in the corners of the eyes, and genuine sentiment nestles in the heart. In more recent times the horizon has widened, and there has been a gain in both breadth of view and depth of insight. Genius and art have combined to make this classic soil.

It is a small section of country, comprising only a few counties, but with them are indelibly associated the names of A. B. Longstreet, W. T. Thompson, J. J. Hooper, Francis O. Ticknor, Richard Malcolm Johnston, Harry Stillwell Edwards, Sidney Lanier, Maurice Thompson, Joel Chandler Harris, and many other less known writers. If we turn to their characters and scenes, the association is still more intimate. Ransy Sniffle and Ned Brace belong to Baldwin, the scene of "The Fight," "The Gander Pulling," and "The Militia Drill." In the woods and along the river banks of the same county "The Two Runaways" were wont at a later day to enjoy their annual escapade. "Simon Suggs" was a native of Jasper; "Major Jones's Courtship" took place in Morgan; "Mr. Absalom Billingslea and Other Georgia Folk" are at home in Hancock; but to Putnam County was awarded the honor of giving birth to "Uncle Remus," a veritable Ethiopian Æsop, philosopher, and gentleman, and to the "Little Boy," whose inexhaustible curiosity and eagerness to hear a "story" have called forth the most valuable and, in the writer's opinion, the most permanent contribution to American literature in the last quarter of this century.

This school of humorists are not

realists at all in the modern sense; for nothing is farther from their writings than sadness, morbidness, and pessimism. Naturalism is the term by which their literary method may best be characterized. They look frankly and hearken attentively, following, at a great distance it may be, Fielding's and the great master's plan of holding the mirror up to nature. But coloring, tone, and substance have been reproduced with such absolute fidelity because the heart is full of hope, the eye bright, and a smile ever playing around the mouth. It is also easy to see that they are to the manner born. "To be sure," says Judge Longstreet, "in writing the 'Georgia Scenes' I have not confined myself to strictly veracious historic detail; but there is scarcely one word from the beginning to the end of the book that is not strictly *Georgian.* The scenes which I describe—as, for instance, 'The Gander Pulling'—occurred at

the very place where I locate them."
Shortly after the appearance of
" The Adventures of Capt. Simon
Suggs," a friend met the original
on the streets of Monticello and
said : " Squire Suggs, do you remember Jonce Hooper — little
Jonce? " " Seems to me I do,"
replied Mr. Suggs. " Well, Squire,
little Jonce has gone and noveled
you." Mr. Suggs looked serious.
" Gone and noveled me? " he exclaimed. " Well, I'll be danged!
Gone and noveled me? What
could 'a possessed him? " Since
the Civil War the " noveling "
process has gone on with enlarged
sympathies and greater success. A
new figure has been added to the
picture, making it more complete—
the negro. With the wider view
has also come greater freedom of
treatment, and no writers in the
South have appreciated this mental
and artistic liberty more than the
Georgians. Each of them has, by
means of the simplicity, humor, and

45

individuality which characterize the
school, made a distinct contribution
to the sum of human interest and
enjoyment. But the most sympathetic, the most original, the truest
delineator of this larger life—its
manners, c u s t o m s, amusements,
dialect, folklore, humor, pathos, and
character—is Joel Chandler Harris.

His birthplace was Eatonton, the
capital of Putnam County, in Middle
Georgia, and the date of his birth
December 9, 1848. S l i g h t bio-
grapical and personal sketches of
him have appeared in the *Critic*,
in *Literature*, and i n t h e *Book
Buyer*, but the best account of his
early life is to be found in "On the
Plantation," one of the most interesting books that Mr. Harris has
written. In this delightful volume
it is not easy to tell "where confession ends and how far fiction em-
broiders truth." But the author has
kindly left it to the reader to "sift
the fact from the fiction, and label
it to suit himself." As has been

said of another romancer, it is not
through the accidental circumstances of his life that he belongs to
history, but through his talent; and
his talent is in his books. Our first
glimpse of Mr. Harris is in the little post office of Eatonton, which is
also a "country store," and much
frequented for both purposes. He
is sitting upon a rickety, old, faded
green sofa, in a corner of which he
used to curl up nearly every day,
reading such stray newspapers as
he could lay his hands on, and
watching the people come and go.
His look betrays shyness and sensitiveness, though it is full of observation. He is reading in a Milledgeville paper the announcement
of a Mr. Turner, whose acquaintance he has recently made, that he
will begin the publication the following Tuesday of a weekly newspaper, to be called the *Countryman*. It is to be modeled after Mr.
Addison's little paper, the *Spectator*, Mr. Goldsmith's little paper,

the *Bee*, and Mr. Johnson's little paper, the *Rambler*. He has heard of these, for he has had a few terms in the Eatonton Academy, and read some of the best books of the eighteenth century. When the "Vicar of Wakefield" is mentioned his eye sparkles, for since he was six years of age that wonderful story has been a stimulus to his imagination, and made him eager to read all books. He is proud of his acquaintance with a real editor, and waits with great impatience for the first issue of the *Countryman*. In the meanwhile we learn that he cannot be called a studious lad, or at any rate that he is not at all fond of the books in his desk at the Eatonton Academy. On the contrary, he is of an adventurous turn of mind, full of all sorts of pranks and capers; and plenty of people in the little town are ready to declare that he will come to some bad end if he is not more frequently dosed with what the old folks call "hickory oil." But he has a strange sympathy with animals of all kinds, especially horses and dogs, and a deeper, tenderer sympathy with all human beings.

At last the first issue arrives, and is read from beginning to end—advertisements and all. The most important thing in it, as it turned out, was the announcement that the editor wanted a boy to learn the printing business. The friendly postmaster furnished pen, ink, and paper, and the lad applied for the place and got it. Mr. Turner lived about nine miles from Eatonton, on a plantation of some two thousand acres, which was well supplied with slaves, horses, dogs, and game of different kinds. He was a lover of books, and had a choice collection of two or three thousand volumes. His wealth also enabled him to conduct the only country newspaper in the world, which he did so successfully that it reached a circulation of nearly two thousand copies. On

the plantation was a pack of well-
trained harriers, with which the little printer hunted rabbits, and a
fine hound or two of the Birdsong
breed, with which he chased the red
fox. With the negroes he learned
to hunt coons, and possums, and
from them he heard those stories
which have since placed their narrator in the list of the immortals.
The printing office sat deep in a
large grove of oaks, full of gray
squirrels which kept the solitary
typesetter company, running about
over the roofs and playing "hide
and seek" like children. From his
window he watched the partridge
and her mate build their artful nest,
observed their coquetries, and from
her mysteriously skillful manner of
drawing one away from her nest or
her young he learned one of his
earliest and most puzzling lessons
in bird craft. The noisy jay, the
hammering woodpecker, and the
vivacious and tuneful mocking bird
lent their accompaniment to the

clicking of the types. At twelve years of age, then, Mr. Harris found himself in this ideal situation for the richest and most healthful development of his talents. Type-setting came easy, and the lad had the dogs to himself in the late afternoon and the books at night, and he made the most of both. The scholarly planter turned him loose to browse at will in his library, only now and then giving a judicious hint. The great Elizabethans first caught his fancy, and quaint old meditative and poetical Sir Thomas Browne became one of his prime favorites, a place he yet holds. He made many friends among the standard authors that only a boy of a peculiar turn of mind would take to his bosom. But no book at any time has ever usurped the place of the inimitable " Vicar of Wakefield " in his affections—Goethe's, Scott's, Irving's, Thackeray's, all humanity's adorable Vicar. Mr. Harris, like Sir Walter, has read it

in youth and in age, and the charm
endures. In a recent paper he
wrote: "The first book that ever
attracted my attention, and the one
that has held it longest, was and is
the 'Vicar of Wakefield.' T h e
only way to describe my experience
with that book is to acknowledge
that I am a crank. It touches me
more deeply, it gives me the ' all-
overs ' more severely than all others.
Its simplicity, its air of extreme
wonderment, have touched and continue to touch me deeply." These
two favorites have since that early
period found worthy rivals in the
Bible and Shakespeare, and he is
specially serious when he talks of
his heroes, Lee, Jackson, and Lincoln. Job, Ecclesiastes, and Paul's
writings are his prime favorites;
but all good books interest him
more or less, though at the present
time an ardent young writer on a
pilgrimage to this shrine would perhaps find Mr. Harris's library as
scantly supplied as Mr. Howells

found Hawthorne's. There are only a few books, but they are the best, and they have been read and reread. Emerson, however, is not of this number; his "queer self-consciousness" and attitude of self-sufficiency have never appealed to him in any winning way. "You cannot expect an uncultured Georgia cracker to follow patiently the convolute diagrams of the oversoul," he will say; adding, with a quizzical smile: "You see I am perfectly frank in this, presenting the appearance of feeling as proud of my lack of taste and culture as a little girl is of her rag doll." But when culture and individuality are united, as he found them in Lowell, they receive his frankest admiration. "Culture is a very fine thing, indeed," he wrote of Mr. Lowell on his seventieth birthday, "but it is never of much account, either in life or in literature, unless it is used as a cat uses a mouse, as a source of mirth and luxury. It is at its finest in this country when it is grafted on the sturdiness that has made the nation what it is, and when it is fortified by the strong common sense that has developed and preserved the republic. This is culture with a definite aim and purpose, . . . and we feel the ardent spirit of it in pretty much everything Mr. Lowell has written." As for the realists, he admires "immensely" what is best in them, though he has no fondness for minute psychological analysis. He likes a story and "human nature, humble, fascinating, plain, common human nature." "A man is known by the company he keeps," is a saying with a wider application, I fancy, than is comly given to it. I had a friend once —a strong, earnest, meditative, silent man—over the m a n t e l in whose study hung a portrait of William Cullen Bryant. The kinship of nature could easily be traced between these two and that great American of whom Bryant wrote:

Joel Chandler Harris.

The wildest storm that sweeps through
    space,
  And rends the oak with sudden force,
Can raise no ripple on his face,
  Or slacken his majestic course.

    I could easily imagine my friend
in the heart of some primeval forest
—he had a deep and reverent love
of nature—repeating his favorite
lines :
            Be it ours to meditate,
In these calm shades, thy milder majesty,
And to the beautiful order of thy works
Learn to conform the order of our lives.

    And so, consciously or unconscious-
ly, Mr. Harris has imbibed old-
fashioned ways of simplicity, naturalness, and truth from his Shakespeare and Bible ; has had ingrained
in the fiber of his being the gentleness, delicacy, and purity of feeling
which distinguish the good Vicar's
author, and has conformed his life
to that sentiment of Sir Thomas
Browne's which " The Autocrat "
considered the most admirable in
any literature : " Every man truly
lives so long as he acts his nature

or some way makes good the faculties of himself."

Among these books he lived for several years, and almost before he knew it he was acquainted with those writers who lend wings to the creative imagination, if its delicate body has found habitation in a human soul. With the acquisition of knowledge went also hand in hand an observation of life and of nature. As he left his native village in the buggy with Mr. Turner, he had observed how quickly his little companions returned to their marbles after bidding him good-bye; and he had observed, too, how the high sheriff was "always in town talking politics," and talking "bigger than anybody." When he came to the plantation his observant eye took in everything, and the observations of the boy became the basis of the lifelong convictions and principles of the man. His greatest nature-gift, sympathy, put him in touch with dog and horse, with

Joel Chandler Harris.

black runaway and white deserter,
with the master and his slaves.
These, he observed, treated him
with more consideration than they
showed to other white people, with
the exception of their master.
There was nothing they were not
ready to do for him at any time of
day or night. Taking him into
their inner life, they poured a
wealth of legendary folklore and
story into his retentive ear, and to
him revealed their true nature; for
it is not a race that plays its tricks,
as some one has said of nature, un-
reservedly before the eyes of everybody.

Mr. Harris has never had the
slightest desire to become a man of
letters; but the necessity of expressing himself in writing came
upon him early in life. His first
efforts appeared in the *Countryman*, sent in anonymously. Kindly
notice and encouragement induced
the young writer to throw off disguise and to write regularly. His

contributions soon took a wider
range, embracing local articles, essays, and poetry. But this idyllic
existence was s u d d e n l y ended.
Sherman's " march t h r o u g h
Georgia" brought a corps of his
army to the Turner plantation, and
when the foragers departed they
left little behind them except a
changed order of things. The
editor-planter called up those of his
former slaves that remained, and
told them that they were free. The
Countryman passed away with the
old order, devising, however, a rich
legacy to the new. "A larger
world beckoned [to the young
writer] and he went out into it.
And it came about that on every
side he found loving hearts to comfort and strong and friendly hands
to guide him. He found new associations, and formed new ties. In
a humble way he made a name for
himself, but the old plantation days
still l i v e in his dreams." The
" Wanderjahre " were few and un-

Joel Chandler Harris.

eventful. Now we find him setting his "string" on the *Macon Daily Telegraph*, then in a few months he is in New Orleans as a private secretary of the editor of the *Crescent Monthly*, keeping his hand in, however, by writing bright paragraphs for the city papers. In a short while he returns to Georgia to become the editor of the *Forsyth Advertiser*, one of the most influential weekly papers in the State. In addition to the editorial work, he set the type, worked off the edition on a hand press, and wrapped and directed his papers for the mail. His bubbling humor and pungent criticism of certain abuses in the State were widely copied, and specially attracted the attention of Colonel W. T. Thompson, the author of "Major Jones's Courtship" and other humorous books, who at that time was editor of the *Savannah Daily News*. He offered Mr. Harris a place on his staff, which was accepted; and this pleasant associa-

tion lasted from 1871 to 1876. In
the latter year a yellow fever epidemic drove him to Atlanta; he
became at once a member of the
editorial staff of the *Constitution*,
and his literary activity began.
And it is altogether fitting, too, that
Mr. Harris's success should be identified with this popular journal, for
no other newspaper published in the
South has given so much attention
to literary matters and encouragement to literary talent. Up to this
time Mr. Harris had written, so far
as I am aware, but one brief little
sketch, a mere incident, which gave
any promise of his future line of
development and peculiar powers.
It appeared in the *Countryman* at
the close of the war—a little sequel
to the passing of the Twentieth
Army Corps, commanded by General Slocum, along the road by the
Turner plantation. Thinking that
the army would take another route,
the lonely lad had seated himself on
the fence, and before he knew it the

troops were upon him. Their good-natured chaff he endured with a kind of stunned calmness till all passed. He then jumped from the fence and made his way home through the fields. "In a corner of the fence, not far from the road, Joe found an old negro woman shivering and moaning. Near her lay an old negro man, his shoulders covered with an old, ragged shawl. 'Who is that lying there?' asked Joe. 'It my ole man, suh.' 'What is the matter with him?' 'He dead, suh; but bless God, he died free!'"

Just before Mr. Harris went to Atlanta Mr. S. W. Small had begun to give the *Constitution* a more than local reputation by means of humorous negro dialect sketches. His resignation shortly afterwards made the proprietors turn for aid to Mr. Harris, who, taking an old negro whom he had known on the Turner plantation and making him chief spokesman, brought out in several sketches the contrast be-

tween the old and the new condition of things. But he soon tired of
these, and one night he wrote the
first sketch in " Legends of the Plantation," in which " Uncle Remus "
initiates the " Little Boy," just as it
now appears in his first published
volume, entitled, " Uncle Remus :
His Songs and Sayings." Fame
came at once, though the invincible
modesty of the author still refuses to
recognize it. A number of things
enhanced the value of this production—the wealth of folklore, the accurate and entertaining dialect, the
delightful stories, the exquisite picture of " the dear remembered days."
But the true secret of the power and
value of " Uncle Remus " and his
" Sayings " does not lie solely in the
artistic and masterly setting and
narration. The enduring quality
lies there, for he has made a past
civilization " remarkably striking to
the mind's eye," and shown that
rare ability " to seize the heart of
the suggestion, and make a country

famous with a legend." But under-
neath the art is the clear view of
life, as well as humor, wit, philosophy, and "unadulterated human nature." We can get little idea of the
revelation which Mr. Harris has
made of negro life and character
without comparing his conception
and delineation with the ideal negro
of "My Old Kentucky Home,"
"Uncle Tom's Cabin," and "Mars
Chan" and "Meh Lady," and the
impossible negro of the minstrel
show. A few years ago the editor
of the *Philadelphia Times* remarked
that "it is doubtful whether the real
negro can be got very clearly into
literature except by way of minstrel
shows and the comic drama." In
answer to this Mr. Harris has truthfully said that "a representation of
negro life and character has never
been put upon the stage, nor anything remotely resembling it; but to
all who have any knowledge of the
negro, the plantation darky, as he
was, is a very attractive figure. It

is a silly trick of the clowns to give him over to burlesque, for his life, though abounding in humor, was concerned with all that the imagination of man has made pathetic." The negro of the minstrel show, black with burnt cork, sleek and saucy, white - eyed, red - lipped, crowned with plug hat, wearing enormous shoes, and carrying a banjo, rises to the dignity of a caricature only in the external appearance. The wit reeks with stale beer and the Bowery. Foster's "My Old Kentucky Home" is simply "Uncle Tom's Cabin" turned into a song; and the latter, says Irwin Russell, "powerfully written as it is, gives no more true idea of negro life and character than one could get from the Nautical Almanac, and, like most other political documents, is quite the reverse of true in almost every respect." These contain the sentiments and the thoughts of artist-philanthropists belonging to a race "three or four thousand years in advance of them [the negroes] in mental capacity and moral force." They do breathe with infinite pathos the homely affection, the sorrows and hopes of everyday life, as these have been developed and conceived by the white race; but who ever heard that this was a favorite song or that a favorite book in any community of negroes? And so Mr. Page's "Marse Chan" and "Meh Lady," and Mr. Allen's "Two Gentlemen of Kentucky," are the answers of genius to genius and art pitted against art in this great controversy. In them the devotion, the doglike fidelity, and the unselfishness of the negro are used to intensify the pathos of the white man's situation, just as in the other case the pathos of the negro's situation was utilized to excite the philanthropy of the white man. In both cases the negro is a mere accessory, used to heighten the effect. It seems to be almost an impossibility for song writer, novelist, or serious historian to appreciate the

nature or understand the condition
of the plantation negroes; for otherwise, how can we account for so
glaring a misconception as Mr.
Bryce's, that they remained, up to
the eve of emancipation, " in their
notions and habits much what their
ancestors were in the forests of the
Niger or the Congo."

The Southern plantation negro
sprang from the child race of humanity, and possessed only so much
civilization as his contact with the
white man gave him. Like children,
he used smiles, cunning, deceit, du-
plicity, ingenuity, and all the other
wiles by which the weaker seek
to accommodate themselves to the
stronger. Brer Rabbit was his hero,
and " it is not virtue that triumphs,
but helplessness; it is not malice,
but mischievousness." In the course
of time he became remarkable for
both inherent and grafted qualities.
Gratitude he was distinguished for;
hospitality and helpfulness were his
natural creed; brutality was con-

spicuously absent, considering the
prodigious depth of his previous
degradation. He did not lack courage, industry, self-denial, or virtue.
He did an immense amount of quiet
thinking, and, with only such forms
of expression as his circumstances
furnished, he indulged in paradox,
hyperbole, aphorism, sententious
comparison, and humor. He treasured his traditions, was enthusiastic,
patient, long-suffering, religious, reverent. "Is there not poetry in the
character?" asked Irwin Russell,
the first, perhaps, to conceive and to
delineate it with real fidelity to life.
Since his all too untimely taking off
many have attempted this subject;
but no one has equaled the creator of "Uncle Remus," one of the
very few creations of American
writers worthy of a place in the
gallery of the immortals; and he
should be hung in the corner with
such gentlemen as Col. Newcome
and Sir Roger de Coverley, and
not very far from Rip Van Win-

kle, my Uncle Toby, and Jack Fal-
staff.

Before the war Uncle Remus had
always exercised authority over his
fellow-servants. He had been the
captain of the corn pile, the stoutest
at the log rolling, the swiftest with
the hoe, the neatest with the plow,
the leader of the plantation hands.
Now he is an old man whose tall
figure and venerable appearance are
picturesque in the extreme, but he
moves and speaks with the vigor of
perennial youth. He is the embodiment of the quaint and homely humor, the picturesque sensitiveness—
a curious exaltation of mind and
temperament not to be defined by
words—and the really poetic imagination of the negro race; and over
all is diffused the genuine flavor of
the old plantation. With the art to
conceal art, the anthor retires behind
the scenes and lets this patriarch reveal negro life and character to the
world. Now it is under the guise
of Brer Rabbit, after his perilous

adventure with the tar baby and narrow escape from Brer Fox as he is seen " settin' cross-legged on a chinkapin log koamin' de pitch outen his har wid a chip," and " flingin' back some er his sass, ' Bred and bawn in a brier patch, Brer Fox; bred and bawn in a brier patch ! ' " Another phase is seen in " Why Brer Possum Loves Peace," a story of indolent good nature, questionable valor, and nonsensical wisdom : " I don' min' fightin' no mo' dan you doz, sez'ee, but I declar' to grashus ef I kin stan' ticklin.' An' down ter dis day," continued Uncle Remus, " down ter dis day, Brer Possum's boun' ter s'render w'en you tech him in de short ribs, en he'll laff ef he knows he's gwine ter be smashed for it." This whimsical defense of inborn cowardice has a touch of nature in it which makes it marvelously akin to Sir John's counterfeiting on Shrewsbury plain. But the prevailing interest is centered in Brer Rabbit's skill in outwitting Brer

Joel Chandler Harris.

Fox and the other animals, which is managed with such cleverness and good nature that we cannot but sympathize with the hero, in spite of his utter lack of conscience or conviction. But the chief merit of these stories, as Mr. Page has remarked, springs directly from the fact that Uncle Remus knows them, is relating them, and is vivifying them with his own quaintness and humor, and is impressing us in every phase with his own delightful and lovable personality. Mr. Harris's skill in narrative is well-nigh perfect, and the conversation, in which his books abound, is carried on with absolute naturalness and fidelity to life. The habit of thought as well as of speech is strikingly reproduced. Not a word strikes a false note, not a scene or incident is out of keeping with the spirit of the life presented. No one has more perfectly preserved some of the most important traits of Southern character, nor more enchantingly presented some of the most beau-

70

tiful phases of Southern civilization.

Other phases of negro character,
very different from those presented in
the "Legends," appeared in the "Sayings" and in various "Sketches,"
which reproduce "the shrewd ob-
ervations, the curious retorts, the
homely thrusts, the quaint comments, and the humorous philosophy
of the race of which Uncle Remus
is a type." But in "Nights with
Uncle Remus," "Daddy Jake the
Runaway," and "Uncle Remus and
His Friends" we returned again to
the old plantation home; "daddy,"
"mammy," and the "field hands"
lived once more with their happy,
smiling faces; songs floated out upon
the summer air, laden with the perfume of rose and honeysuckle and
peach blossom, and mingled with
the rollicking medley of the mocking bird; and we felt that somehow
over the whole life the spell of genius had been thrown, rendering it
immortal. But it is with and through

the negro that Mr. Harris has
wrought this wonder, for as Mr.
Page says : "No man who has ever
written has known one-tenth part
about the negro that Mr. Harris
knows, and for those who hereafter
shall wish to find not merely the
words, but the real language of the
negro of that section, and the habits
of mind of all American negroes of
the old time, his works will prove
the best thesaurus."

Again a larger world beckoned to
the writer, as to the boy, and he entered the field of original story-telling and wider creative ability with
perfect poise and consummate literary art in "Mingo," a "Cracker"
tragedy, disclosing the pent-up rage
of a century against aristocratic
neighbors, antipathy to the negro,
narrowness and pride, happily turned
by Mingo's gratitude and watchful
and protecting love for his young
"Mistiss's" fatherless and mother-
less little girl into a smiling comedy,
closing with this pretty picture :

"The sunshine falling gently upon his gray hairs, and the little girl clinging to his hand and daintily throwing kisses." Mingo, drawn with genuine sympathy and true skill, is one of the author's master-pieces; but we are somehow specially attracted to Mrs. Feratia Bivins, whose "pa would 'a' bin a rich man, an' 'a' owned *niggers*, if it hadn't but 'a' bin bekase he sot his head agin stintin' of his stomach," and whose sharp tongue, homely wit, and indignant hate portray the first of a group of the Mrs. Poyser-like women who give spice as well as life to the author's pages. Another is Mrs. Kendrick in "Blue Dave"—of which, by the bye, the author says, "I like 'Blue Dave' better than all the rest, which is another way of saying that it is far from the best"—whose humor conceals her own emotions, and flashes a calcium light upon the weaknesses of others. "Well, well, well!" said Mrs. Kendrick, speaking of the quiet, self-contained, elegant, and rather prim Mrs. Denham. "She always put me in mind of a ghost that can't be laid on account of its pride. But we're what the Lord made us, I reckon, and people deceive their looks. My old turkey gobbler is harmless as a hound puppy, but I reckon he'd bust if he didn't up and strut when strangers are in the front porch." "Uncle Remus," "Mingo," "Blue Dave," and "Balaam" belong to the class which "has nothing but pleasant memories of the discipline of slavery, and which has all the prejudices of caste and pride of family that were the natural results of the system." But "Free Joe" presents another phase—this heart tragedy brought about by the inhumanity of man and the pitiless force of circumstances. Nowhere has the helpless wretchedness of the dark side of slavery been more clearly recognized or more powerfully depicted. Truth demands that the complete picture shall be given, though silly scribbler or narrow bigot may accuse the author of trying to cater to Northern sentiment. Every now and then some Southern writer is subjected to this unmanly and ignoble insult, though much less frequently than formerly. Mr. Maurice Thompson's poem and Mr. Henry Watterson's speech on "Lincoln," Mr. James Lane Allen's lecture on "The South in Fiction," and Mr. W. P. Trent's "Life of William Gilmore Simms," seem to produce a mild form of rabies in certain quarters. "What does it matter," asks Mr. Harris, "whether I am Northern or Southern, if I am true to truth, and true to that larger truth, my own true self? My idea is that truth is more important than sectionalism, and that literature that can be labeled Northern, Southern, Western, or Eastern is not worth labeling at all." Shutting one's eyes to facts removes them neither from life nor from history. And so we are specially thankful to Mr. Harris for

"Free Joe," "Little Compton," and
all those passages in "On the Plantation" and his other writings which
lead us to a truer and larger humanity. His skillful manner of conveying a lesson is admirably done at the
close of "Free Joe." This "black
atom drifting hither and thither without an owner, blown about by all the
winds of circumstance, and given
over to shiftlessness," is the personification of helpless suffering, and
yet he chuckles as he slips away
from the cabin of the cracker brother and sister into the night. Micajah
Staley, however, the representative
of too large a number, says : "Look
at that nigger; look at 'im. He's
pine blank as happy now as a kildee
by a mill race. You can't 'faze 'em.
I'd in about give up my t'other hand
ef I could stan' flat-footed an' grin
at trouble like that there nigger."
"Niggers is niggers," said Miss
Becky, smiling grimly, "an' you
can't rub it out; yit I lay I've seed
a heap of white folks lots meaner'n

Joel Chandler Harris.

Free Joe. He grins—and that's nigger—but I've ketched his underjaw
a trimblin' when Lucindy's name uz
brung up." He was found dead the
next morning, with a smile on his face.
" It was as if he had bowed and
smiled when death stood before him,
humble to the last." The world could
ill spare woman's or the artist's eye.

Other stories, as "At Teague Poteet's," " Trouble on Lost Mountain," and "Azalia," show a steady
gain in the range of Mr. Harris's
creative power. The keenest interest was awakened when the first
part of "At Teague Poteet's " came
out in the *Century*, May, 1883, and
the reader who happened to turn to
the *Atlantic* for the same month
and read " The Harnt That Walks
Chilhowee " must have been sur-
prised at the revelation which these
two admirable stories made of the
real and potent romance of the mountains and valleys of Tennessee and
Georgia. This was a longer and
more sustained effort than Uncle

Remus had ever attempted. It evinced an eye for local color, appreciation of individual characteristics, and the ability to catch the spirit of a people that could be as open as their valleys or as rugged, enigmatical, and silent as their mountains. Scene and character were vividly real, and the story was told with consummate art and unflagging interest till the climax was reached. "Trouble on Lost Mountain" sustained his reputation as a story-teller and added the element of tragic power.

At a first glance it would seem that these, with his previous writings, give promise of the fully developed novel with the old plantation life for a background and the nation for its scope. But it must not be forgotten that Mr. Harris is a hard-working journalist, seldom missing a day from his desk; and as Mr. Stedman has pointed out in regard to Bayard Taylor, "this task of daily writing for the press,

while a good staff, is a poor crutch ;
it diffuses the heat of authorship,
checks idealism, retards the construction of masterpieces." It is perhaps
due to this that the love element in
these stories lacks that romantic fervor and tenderness which make all
the world love a lover. They are
vivid and dramatic, sparkling with
humor and keen observations, and
revealing intimate knowledge of human hearts. But in "Azalia," for
instance, the Southern general and
his mother are rather conventional,
and Miss Hallie is insipid, though
through them we do catch glimpses
of old Southern mansions, with their
stately yet simple architecture, admirably illustrative of the lives and
characters of the owners, and of the
unaffected, warm, and gracious old-
time hospitality. The Northern ladies, too, admirably described as
they are in a few words, are slight
sketches rather than true presentments. This story is particularly
rich in types, but the real life in its

humor and its pathos is in the "characters." Mrs. Haley, a lineal descendant of Mrs. Poyser; William, a little imp of sable hue that might serve as a weather-stained statue of comedy, if he were not so instinct with life; and Emma Jane Stucky —the representative of that indescribable class of people known as the piny woods " Tackies "—whose " pale, unhealthy-looking face, with sunken eyes, high cheek-bones, and thin lips that seemed never to have troubled themselves to smile — a burnt-out face that had apparently surrendered to the past and had no hope for the future "—remains indelibly etched upon the memory, making its mute appeal for human sympathy and helpful and generous pity. Like all genuine humorists, Mr. Harris has his wit always seasoned with love, and a moral purpose underlies all his writings. In the twelve volumes or more which he has published he has preserved traditions and legends, photographed a civilization, perpetuated types, created one character. Humor and sympathy are his chief qualities, and in everything he is simple and natural. Human character is stripped of tireless details. The people speak their natural language, and act out their little tragedies and comedies according to their nature. "We see them, share their joys and griefs, laugh at their humor, and in the midst of all, behold, we are taught the lesson of honesty, justice, and mercy."

In person Joel Chandler Harris is somewhat under the middle height, compact, broad of shoulder, and rather rotund about the waist. But he is supple, energetic, and his swinging stride still tells of the freedom which the boy enjoyed on the Turner plantation. He is the most pronounced of blondes, with chestnut hair, a mustache of the same color, and sympathetic, laughing blue eyes. Sick or well, he is always in a good humor, and enjoys his work, his friends, and his family. Sprung

from a simple, sincere race whose
wants were few and whose tastes
were easily satisfied, he is very honest and outspoken in his opinions
and convictions, and the whole nature of the man tends to earnestness,
simplicity, and truth. "I like people," he says, "who are what they
are, and are not all the time trying
to be what somebody else has been."
In spite of the fame which has come
unbidden, he still delights to luxu-
riate in the quiet restfulness of his
semirural home in the little suburb
of West End, three miles from the
heart of Atlanta ; and we confess that
we like best to think of him, as Mr.
Brainerd once described him in the
Critic, in this typical Southern cottage nestling in a grove of sweet
gum and pine, enlivened by the singing of a family of mocking birds that
wintered in his garden—and not a
bird among them, we imagined, with
whose peculiarities he was not familiar. In a distant corner of his
inclosure a group of brown-eyed

Joel Chandler Harris.

Jerseys grazed. Hives of bees were placed near a flower garden that sloped down to the bubbling spring at the foot of the road, a few rods distant. The casual visitor, we were told, was apt to be eyed by the dignified glance of a superb English mastiff, followed by the bark of two of the finest dogs in the country—one a bull dog, the other a white English bull terrier. But this was published in 1885, and now Mr. Garsney, in the *Book Buyer* for March, 1896, tells us that the " grove of sweet gums," the " babbling brook," and the " droning bees are all fictions of somebody else's poetic fancy." Still Mr. Garsney, in his setting for the author of " Uncle Remus," has the eye of an artist and is himself full of poetry, however ruthless he may be with " poetic fancies," for after placing him " amid his roses," he adds : " The roses are his one passion, and under his tender care the garden—the finest rose garden in Atlanta outside of a

83

florist's domain—blooms with prodigal beauty from May until the middle of December. In the early summer mornings, when the mocking birds are trying their notes in the cedar, and the wrens are chirping over their nest in the old mail box at the gate, you can hear the snipping of the pruning shears, and you know that Joel Chandler Harris is caressing his roses while the dew is yet on their healthy leaves."

In this home, with its spacious verandas, generous hearths, and wide, sunny windows, the right man is sure to find a welcome. The house is one in which bric-a-brac, trumpery, and literary litter are conspicuously absent, but evidently a home where wife and children take the place of these inanimate objects of devotion. But here the man Joel Chandler Harris, as Carlyle would have said, is seen at his best. It is here that the usually silent or monosyllabic figure takes on life and shares with another his inner wealth of thought and fancy. Mr. Garsney, who had the good fortune to be an inmate of this home for some months, and to whose sketch the writer is indebted for many of these personal remarks and observations, thus describes certain rare moments : " It is in the darkness of a summer evening, on the great front porch of his house, or by his fireside, with no light save that from the flickering coals which he loves to punch and caress, that the man breaks forth into conversation. I have had in these rare twilight hours the plot of a whole book unfolded to me—a book that is yet in the dim future, but which will make a stir when it appears ; I have heard stories innumerable of old plantation life and of happenings in Georgia during the war ; and I have heard through the mouth of this taciturn and unliterary-looking man more thrilling stories of colonial life in the South than I had believed the South held. At

these times the slight hesitancy that
is usually apparent in his speech disappears; his thoughts take words
and come forth, tinged by the quaint
Georgia dialect, in so original a
shape and so full of human nature
that one remembers these hours long
afterwards as times to be marked
with a white stone."

But it is only to the chosen companion that he thus unlocks his
treasures. He seldom has more
than a word for ordinary acquaint-
ances, and the ubiquitous interview-
er he avoids as a deadly plague.
From him the autograph fiends
get no response, and many amusing stories are told of his success in eluding sightseers and lion-
hunters. No inducement has yet
prevailed upon him to appear in
public, either as a reader or as a lec-
turer. "I would not do it for $1,-
000,000," was once his response to
an invitation to lecture. Many po-
sitions of great trust and prominence,
we are told, have been refused by

him, for he says : " If the greatest
position on the round earth were to
be offered me, I wouldn't take it.
The responsibility would kill me in
two weeks. Now I haven't any care
or any troubles, and I have resolved
never to worry any more. Life is
all a joke to me. Why make it a
care?"

To those who are engaged in the
pigmy contests for money and place
this philosophy will doubtless appear tame and unheroic. But for a
man of Mr. Harris's peculiar gifts
and temperament it is the highest
wisdom. It means the saving for
mankind what a few would squan-
der upon themselves. It means more
inimitable stories, and since his success in the past justifies us in expecting it, and especially since he has
reached the age of ripest wisdom
and supremest effort on the part of
genius, it means, we may hope,
a work into which he will put
the wealth of his mind and heart,
and expand and compress into one

novel the completest expression of his whole being. But if he should never give us a masterpiece of fiction like his beloved " Vicar of Wakefield," "Ivanhoe," " Vanity Fair," or " The Scarlet Letter," we shall still be forever grateful for the fresh and beautiful stories, the delightful humor, the genial, manly philosophy, and the wise and witty sayings in which his writings abound. His characters have become world possessions; his words are in all our mouths. By virtue of these gifts he will be enrolled in that small but distinguished company of humorists, the immortals of the heart and home, whose genius, wisdom, and charity keep fresh and sweet the springs of life, and Uncle Remus will live always.

88

Maurice Thompson.

———

THE greatest writers cannot agree in defining genius. No university has ever framed a course of study adapted to its varied and peculiar wants. For my part, I am glad that scholars had no chance to put Jonson's "learned sock" on "sweetest Shakespeare, fancy's child." Was it not fortunate that Burns's head was filled with stories of warlocks and witch-es, with ballads and old wives' fa-bles, instead of Latin nouns, Greek verbs, and mathematical problems? Suppose Scott's school reputation was one of irregular ability, and Wordsworth would read Richard-son's novels when he should have been cramming for examination; granted that Thackeray's school-fellows, peering over his shoulder,

did always find him making humorous and fantastic sketches from Homer, from Horace, from Scott's poems, from Cooper's novels (he seldom had any other kind of books in
his hand then), and that Bunyan
had only two books in his library—
did not each in the end get that education which suited him best and
enriched the world most? Ever and
anon there comes a time when our
poets must touch mother earth and
grow strong again. In this way literature becomes fresher and sweeter
and loses that bookishness which
handicaps Pegasus, though Milton
or George Eliot be the rider. Is it
an unhealthy sign that so many of
our younger writers are not college
bred? Those of the Southern school
had small chance to get a collegiate
education. But they grew up at a
time and amid surroundings that fitted them far better to create a new,
fresh, and original literature. A
typical example is the subject of this
sketch. Although he has not com-

monly been classed with the Southern school, there is not one of them
more distinctly Southern in his lin-
eage, his life, and his writings. He
was reared in the South. His writings have the freshness and fragrance of the South. In conception
and coloring they are distinctly
Southern, and oftentimes there is
even a tropical glow in his creations.
Though his home is in Indiana, he
has spent almost every winter of his
life either in Florida or on the gulf
coast, nowadays usually at Bay St.
Louis. He has thus ever kept in
touch and sympathy with Southern
life and effort, and had close companionship with Southern sky and
sea and wood and bird.

Maurice Thompson was born at
Fairfield, Ind., September 9, 1844,
where his father was temporarily
residing. His family on the father's
side comes of Scotch-Irish stock, and
on the mother's side it is Dutch, but
both paternal and maternal ancestors
fought in the patriot army during

the Revolution, some under Lafay-
ette, some under Francis Marion in
the Carolinas. Four generations
ago we find the great-great-grand-
father of Maurice Thompson a companion of Daniel Boone in the Indian wars of Kentucky, the family,
of Irish descent, having come to the
"bloody hunting grounds" from
Virginia. The son of this Thompson was a Baptist minister, well
known in the early days of Ohio and
Indiana. About seventy years ago
he sat in the Indiana Legislature, and
later was nominated by his party for
Congress, but defeated by a few
votes. The preacher - politician's
wife was a daughter of a Revolutionary soldier, of Scotch descent.
Their son, Maurice's father, was born
in Missouri, and in due time he too
became a Baptist minister. Though
not in the strictest sense an educated
man, he was an orator of real power,
and he wrote books of a doctrinal
sort that were long popular with
his denomination. He lived to a good

old age, dying in March, 1888, about
seventy-seven years old.

Mr. Thompson's mother was born
in New York, and her maiden name
was Jägger. Her father, of Dutch
origin, was a soldier in the war of
1812, and the family moved to Indiana in 1818. She is well educated,
and a great lover of the best books.
"To her," the son says, "I owe
everything. Her intimate knowledge of the best English literature,
especially that of Shakespeare, Scott,
Byron, Shelley, and Keats, was early impressed upon me. From childhood to manhood she was my boon
companion, my playmate, my adviser, my teacher, my loving and
encouraging critic, my everything—
my mother!" She lives with him
now, in her eighty-third year, and
enjoys the rare fortune of still having not only a perfect mind, but an
unabated relish for all good reading.

Shortly after his birth his parents
removed to Missouri, and settled in
the woods of the Southeastern part

of that State. Returning to Indiana, they went thence to Kentucky, where they remained until he was nine or ten years of age, and then continued their southward flight till they nestled in the beautiful valley of the Coosawattee, a little stream of North Georgia. Here his father bought a plantation in a fertile but lonely place, and for several years he lived, to use his own words, "a sweet, wild life, hard enough in many respects, almost savage in some—a sweet, wild life, as I remember it, however, devoted to books, manual labor, wildwood roaming, shooting, and fishing." Later his life was the "most picturesque, no doubt, that has befallen any American youth." This he has promised to give us some time or other. He became practically a denizen of the woods, bearing about with him in his rambles books and shooting implements —sometimes a gun, sometimes a bow and arrows. He made long voyages in a canoe, journeys into Florida and along the gulf coast; he climbed mountains and explored swamps. "At first," he says, " I was conscious of no fixed aim—had no definite purpose. I was impelled to go into the wilds of nature, and went. But as my experience broadened I began to feel all my myriad scraps of knowledge, s n a t c h e d here from books and there from nature, fusing in the heat of my imagination and running together in a strong current toward the outlet of literary expression."

How he obtained an education it would be difficult even for him to tell, the sources have been so manifold. A poet absorbs knowledge through every spiritual pore, from every influence of life, every vent of nature. The beautiful valley of the Saliquoy, nearly midway between Atlanta and Chattanooga, where the family found a home, was at that time so remote from the world that no good school was within reach. His father was much away from home, and, though private tutors were employed from time to time, the boy's education was really directed by his mother. But from mother and tutors he received good instruction in Greek, in Latin, in French, in German, in Hebrew, in mathematics — his favorite study, of which he has always been passionately fond, and for which he has such affinity that he has never had any trouble in its study at all—and in the English poets. He studied Kant, Leibnitz, and Spinoza in a way, worshiped Poe for awhile, then idolized Victor Hugo in a boyish abandon, got the " Somnium Scipionis " by heart, and lost himself in the Greek lyrists. Part of this was before and part after the Civil War, but even during his soldier life he was studying and reading. While stationed at Thunderbolt, near Savannah, Ga., he enjoyed " La Nouvelle Héloïse " for the first time, and here and there in camp he read Carlyle's essays, De

Maurice Thompson.

Quincey's works, and other fine
literature. While serving as a scout
in 1864 he was chided by his supe-
riors for carrying about with him
one of Hugh Miller's works.

In a " Boys' Book of Sports " he
has told us how he prosecuted his
studies in boyhood. " I wished to
study all the branches of a liberal
education," says he, " while paying
special attention to zoology and
general natural history; and I so
arranged my studies that by spend-
ing more than the usual time with
my teachers Mondays, Tuesdays,
and Wednesdays, I had Thursdays,
Fridays, and Saturdays free for my
woodland ramblings and outdoor
studies. It was a very joyful school
life. While lying beside clear mountain springs in the cool shade of the
wild woods, with many rare songsters warbling above me, I read
Wilson and Bonaparte and Audu-
bon's books on birds. At other
times I would sit on the cedar-cov-
ered bluffs of the Coosawattee and

pore over mathematical problems.
I read some choice novels, principal-
ly French, in order to get a good
knowledge of that language. I remember well how the 'Romance of
a Poor Young Man' delighted me.
I translated and read, during one
bass-fishing season, the 'Essay on
Old Age' and the 'Somnium Scipionis' of Cicero, and many of the
odes of Horace."

This school life in the woods was
made more delightful by the companionship of a younger brother
who studied with him. This brother was an enthusiastic egg hunter,
and collected for the cabinets of two
or three gentlemen a great number
of rare bird eggs. Both took great
delight in shooting with the bow
and arrow. "As I look back upon
this life now," he says, "it appears
curiously confused—a sort of *pot-
pourri* of study and play and
dreaming, content and discontent—
an odd jumble indeed." But it was
this manner of life which differen-

tiated him from other writers, and
which has made his writings so
characteristic. The origin of his
theory of criticism is not far to
seek. "Outdoor Influences in Literature," "Tangle - leaf Papers,"
every chapter in " By - ways and
Bird - notes " and in "Sylvan Secrets " give evidence of the "richer
reward " obtainable from the " living, budding, redolent, resonant byways of our neighborhoods." In
such company " even Poe and Hawthorne disclose too heavy a trace of
the must and mold of the closet."
There is " lacking that balmy, odorous freshness of the morning woods
and pastures, when the convolvulus
and the violets are in bloom.

The skies they were ashen and sober,
The leaves they were crisp and sere,

in all their writings."

In another place he says : " To
study nature is the surest way to a
knowledge of what art ought to be.
Nature is the standard. I have
little respect for the judgment of

the critic who measures one man's work by that of another. The main question, when any art work is critically considered, should be: Has it the symmetry, force, and vital beauty of nature?" Again and again he recurs to this thought, and expresses it best perhaps in these words: "The higher forms of art which we have agreed to call creative must get the germs of all new combinations from the suggestions of nature. I have often thought that even criticism in our country would have more virility in it if the critics had more time and more inclination to study nature outside of cities and greenhouses. How can Wordsworth be studied with true critical insight by one who but vaguely remembers the outlines of the woods and the fields, the shady lanes, and the fine aerial effects of hilly landscape? When one with open eyes and ears goes out into the unshorn ways of nature in the creative season — spring — the fine fervor at work in birds and trees and plants, in the air, the earth, and the water is so manifest that one cannot doubt that some subtle element of originality is easily obtainable therefrom by infection."

To return to his life : Mr. Thompson entered the Southern army in 1862, and was honorably surrendered at Kingston, Ga., in May, 1865. As to his feelings regarding the struggle between the North and the South in the war he was conscientiously on the side of the South; still, toward the close of the fight, as he grew older and more thoughtful, he began to see that human slavery was an unmitigated evil, and that the constitution of the Confederate States was without inherent value—without power to hold the States together, and without any central idea upon which patriotism could focus itself. About the same time Georgia was talking of secession. But then, as now, he was "passionately attached" to the

South and he "stayed with her till
the fight closed." "But for the
last year of the struggle," Mr.
Thompson says, "the feeling was
growing in me that we were bat-
tling against the nineteenth century,
and that even if we whipped the
North we could not drive back the
whole phalanx of progress."

In the closing lines of his poem,
" To the South," which he addresses as

Land where our Washington was born,
When truth in hearts of gold was worn;
Mother of Marion, Moultrie, Lee,
Widow of fallen chivalry!

we have the expression of his ma-
ture conviction in regard to the great
underlying cause of the strife:

I am a Southerner;
I love the South: I dared for her
To fight from Lookout to the sea,
With her proud banner over me:
But from my lips thanksgiving broke,
As God in battle thunder spoke,
And that Black Idol, breeding drouth
And dearth of human sympathy
Throughout the sweet and sensuous
South,

Was, with its chains and human yoke,
Blown hellward from the cannon's mouth,
While Freedom cheered behind the smoke.

But he entered the conflict and fought to the finish with all of a young man's ardor and impetuosity. Wherever he served he was an enthusiastic soldier, an excellent scout, a reckless rider, a fine shot. One of his daring feats has been described by an eyewitness, as follows:

It was once my fortune to see a young man take an ax in his hand and walk alone across two hundred yards of open ground, under the fire of four hundred dismounted troopers, and deliberately cut down a telegraph pole. While he was chopping away at the tough cedar wood I could plainly see the splinters whirling away from the pole from top to bottom as the whizzing bullets aimed at him crashed through it or seamed its side with rugged scars. Near by stood a brick chimney, where a house had been burned down. A twelve-pound shot struck the pile, and it went tumbling to earth, scattering its bricks about, some of them striking the young soldier's legs. He did not waver. As regular as the beat of a pendulum was the swing of that ax, and when the pole fell friends and foes vied together in yelling their admiration of the young man, as he deliberately shouldered his ax and returned to his place in his command.

The motives and passions which hurled him into the war, as well as some of its experiences then and after, have never been more strongly presented than in his poem, "An Address, by an Ex-Confederate Soldier to the Grand Army of the Republic," specially in the following lines :

And was it wrong
To wear the gray my father wore?
Could I shrink back, though young and
strong,
From foes before my mother's door?

My mother's kiss was hot with fight,
My father's frenzy filled his son,
Through reeking day and sodden night
My sister's courage urged me on.

And I, a missile steeped in hate,
Hurled forward like a cannon ball
By the resistless hand of fate,
Rushed wildly, madly through it all.

I stemmed the level flames of hell,
O'er bayonet's bars of death I broke,

Maurice Thompson.

I was so near when Cleburne fell,
  I heard the muffled bullet stroke!

And then his picture of the close, in the same poem, is equally strong and pathetic :

My mother, gray and bent with years,
  Hoarding love's withered aftermath,
Her sweet eyes burnt too dry for tears,
  Sat in the dust of Sherman's path.

My father, broken, helpless, poor,
  A gloomy, nerveless giant stood—
Too strong to cower and endure,
  Too weak to fight for masterhood.

My boyhood's home a blackened heap,
  Where lizards crawled and briers grew.
Had felt the fire of vengeance creep
  The crashing round shot hurtle thro'.

I had no country, all was lost,
  I closed my eyes and longed to die,
While past me stalked the awful ghost
  Of mangled, murdered Liberty.

In this condition the end of the struggle found him. His father still owned two plantations, on one of which the family struggled along till the spring of 1868. During these three years manual labor alternated with hard study. Needing a Greek lexicon and some engineering works, he shot squirrels and sold them at ten cents each for money to buy the books with. In his library are other books bought with money earned in this way. A trough was dug in a large log in which apples from the old orchard were pounded, and in a rude press of his own make he squeezed out the cider and sold it. "The books," he says tenderly, "are sweeter and more fragrant to me now than any cider." His studying was done mostly at night—not by lamp or candle, for he had neither, but by the light of pine knots burning in the fireplace. This was, however, not such a hardship as it may seem, for he had long before learned to study by the "lightwood" flame around the hunters' and the soldiers' camp fires.

While working as a field laborer by day and reviewing his engineering studies by night he thought he saw a prospect for success at law. So with characteristic energy he

Maurice Thompson.

dropped everything else and prepared himself for the practice. But
just when he was opening an office
at Calhoun, Ga., the reconstruction
trouble upset all law. A friend
chanced to advise him to go North,
and in sheer desperation he went,
pulling up at Crawfordsville, Ind.,
"absolutely penniless." Hearing of
a railway survey, he went to the
chief engineer and applied for a
place and received it, with pay at
seventy-five dollars a month. In a
short while he became chief engineer of a railroad, with a salary
of three hundred dollars a month.
He then served as chief engineer in
the construction of several railroads
and other public works. But after
he had saved several hundred dollars he began to practice law, and
was successful from the first. In
a few years he built up a large and
lucrative practice. In the meanwhile
he began to mingle with politicians,
served in the Indiana Legislature,
and became a prominent figure in
107

Maurice Thompson.

State Conventions, and in 1888 was a delegate to the Democratic Na· tional Convention

During all this time, however, nearly since childhood, he had at intervals spurted out this or that essay or hasty puff of song. Horace Greeley, whose acquaintance he had made published some of his poems and stories in the *Tribune*. But his literary life fairly began in 1873, with contributions to the *Atlantic*. These were some lyrics so Greek in their unaffected simplicity and sincerity as to occasion some questionings But Lowell liked them, as well as Mr. Howells, the editor, and years afterwards he wrote Mr. Thompson a characteristic letter, saying " that one of those little poems had rung in his memory ever since like the humming of bees in June." Longfellow welcomed him as a " new and original singer, fresh, joyous, and true," and both Bryant and Emerson took pains to give him strong encouragement. This en·

couragement strengthened his inclination, and in 1880 he set about a literary career in earnest. Four years later he gave up the practice of law to devote himself wholly to letters and science, for he still clung to his scientific studies, and in 1885 he was made State Geologist of Indiana. Since 1889 he has been literary editor of the *New York Independent*; but the publisher of that great journal has given him absolute freedom to go where he pleases—a roving commission—so that, in fact, the heaviest drudgery of editorial life does not fall upon him. Nearly all of his literary essays now appear in the *Independent;* but he is still a regular contributor to the *Century,* and writes occasionally for other magazines.

Mr. Thompson's summer home, "Sherwood Place," is a large and substantial brick house, built somewhat after the style of Southern colonial mansions. It stands in the midst of some acres of old forest

trees and blue grass, and commands
a broad view of Crawfordsville, a
beautiful little town of about ten
thousand inhabitants, noted for its
excellent society, its fine schools, and
its charming homes. The drives and
the streets are superb. Here he began to live in 1871, about the time
of his marriage to Miss Alice Lee,
who has since been all to him that
his mother was before his marriage.
A quiet, modest little woman, refined and cultured, every moment in
her presence increases one's esteem
and admiration for her and shows
that her husband's cheerfulness and
enthusiasm are influenced no less by
his home life than by his outdoor
studies and recreations. Their life
is simple. In summer hammocks
are swung in the trees shading a
lawn set with blue grass, and the
family live much in the open air.
Their children, one son and two
daughters, have grown up, the oldest daughter married and the son
graduated from college and entered

life. The chief room of the house is the library—a place for comfort and study, plain in its appointments, but large, airy, and with deep bay windows in front. Shelves, tables, corners, floor, and even chairs are heaped with books and magazines, not in confusion, but arranged for use. French novels and scientific tomes lie affectionately side by side. Here Mr. Thompson and his wife work together, she reading aloud or writing from his dictation. Mrs. Thompson draws and colors well, and often when he is too busy for this kind of work she sketches outlines of such things as he wishes to remember. Many a time have they sketched together in the Southern or Western woods, and these sketches he finds the best possible suggestions for essays, stories, and poems. For at no time has he ceased to study books and to run at large with nature. No pressing business has ever prevented him from keeping abreast of contemporary science and litera-

Maurice Thompson.

ture; and with Walt Whitman he might say,

I think I have blown with you, O winds;
O waters, I have fingered every shore
    with you;

for, since he went to Indiana in 1868 he has spent some part of every year in the wild woods or wilderness swamps or along the Gulf coast, "by grassy brinks and shady shores," or neath "gloomy, moss-hung cypress grove." Savage life has a fascination for him. He delights "to meet Nature face to face, to put his hand familiarly against her cheek, and to talk to her as an equal." And Nature has treated him kindly, for she has given him his brightest, aptest metaphors, and his freshest, most original thoughts. They glisten and sparkle in his writings like dewdrops. Scintillations of fancy and of thought fly out from every page. She has endowed him, moreover, with never-failing cheerfulness and irrepressible enthusiasm, which make him the most delightful of companions.

He sings, and his is Nature's voice—
   A gush of melody sincere
From that great fount of harmony
   Which thaws and runs when spring is
     here.

Mr. Thompson happily exemplifies Carlyle's saying about poetry, for his eyes see it everywhere. A poetic glamour is thrown over all that he beholds. A poetic fervor suffuses all his writings. Walking through the woods, he sees that where a tree has fallen and decayed there the most beautiful wild flowers grow. We have all noticed such things; but we have not all written the closing lines of "A Prelude:"

And when I fall, like some old tree,
And subtle change makes mold of me,
There let earth show a fertile line
Whence perfect wild flowers leap and
   shine.

Reminiscences and observations are artistically woven into the woof of his prose, and lend to it one of its chiefest charms. Speaking of "some

sweet twitterings in the south of
France which told where the human songsters were hidden," he il-
lustrates the thought with this rem-
iniscence: "Once in the course of
my outdoor life I was sleeping in a
hammock in the midst of a wild
Southern wood. It was late in April,
and the night, though dark, was
stormy, and the sky was like a vast
blessing flung from the hand of God.
I awoke. The stillness and the wood-
shadows were oppressive. Once in
awhile a bird twittered faintly and
dreamily in its sleep, but the profound solitude was not relieved.
Long I lay and felt the loneliness.
Slowly night drew on and on toward morning. Presently a mocking bird awoke and trilled four or
five strange, liquid notes as if half
in fear, half in awe of the wide silence and brooding gloom. Off in
the distance another bird answered.
Then a streak of dawn was flung up
in the east and I knew day was at
hand." Again: "Greek culture and

imagination, stealing westward and northward, was like the march of springtime across the land. It set men and women to singing like birds, it sweetened their souls, fertilized their minds, and blew their lives into passionate bloom." Nor is he less happy in writing of men and books and literary theories. The same freshness and breath of early morn is everywhere apparent. "Vulgar stylists" and "smart analysts" are his abomination. "It was little Horace," he says, "not big Homer, who set such value on the details of verse making." In the midst of his prose, always charming and even exhilarating, he mounts up and carols out some exquisite fancy like this: "Indeed, even nature is not a realist of the analytical, microscopic sort in her best work, for she is not content with showing things just as they are, but must hang a luminous atmosphere about them and touch them with heavenly colors. She knows the blue enchantment of

115

distance, the value of romantic suggestions, the power of dim lines and
mysterious shadows. She sketches
here, she indicates an effect yonder,
at one moment finishing the minutest
details, at another dashing a form-
less wonder on sky or sea or mountain side, but she never stops to
analyze motives or to call attention
to her methods."

His first volume, " Hoosier Mosa-
ics," appeared in 1875—a slight effort giving only here and there, in
the love of birds and of nature, in
close observation, or in some rippling,
sparkling sentence, a promise of the
charming essays, the delightful romances, and the exquisite poems
that were to follow. His second
book, the " Witchery of Archery,"
was more fortunate, and gave him
at least wide notoriety. Archery
clubs were formed almost everywhere, and for awhile it seemed as
if the fashion of shooting with bow
and arrow would grow into a custom. But the intrinsic merits of the

book were apart from the sport.
The sportsman showed that he was
also a keen-eyed observer and a literary artist. The love of nature, the
infinite delight in the wild woods,
swamps, lakes, and mountains, the
personal affection for bird, beast,
and fish, and his genius for description—these were for the first time
made known. With this publication his literary fame began.

But his trips to the South brought
forth other fruit. His eyes began to
note the changes that were rapidly
taking place in social and political life.
He embodied his studies in several
romances: "A Tallahassee Girl,"
"His Second Campaign," and "At
Love's Extremes." The atmosphere in these novels is purely
Southern—air, sunshine, and landscape, too. But in the subtler and
more difficult creations he has not
succeeded so well. Perhaps this
transition period was too evanes-
cent, and he did not go far enough
back into the past. What a field

for romance lies here! The old
plantation home, the hospitable, masterful old Southerner, the creole, the
cracker, the mountaineer, the negro, the cotton, sugar, and rice fields,
the lagoons with long, funereal moss,
the noble pine and stately oak forests, orange groves, magnolia bowers; add to these the sad, grand
story of the war, and what material
and what a setting do all these
things present! Perhaps the real
future historian of the South is to
be a Scott, and the " Wizard of the
South " is destined to have a name
only second to the " Wizard of the
North." Mr. Thompson was one
of the first to recognize this rich
field for romance. He endeavored
to put the old Southerner with his
environment on canvas, to give a
true picture of Southern men and
women and life before the conditions under which they existed
should have utterly passed away.
Here was " a class, to say truth,
with as few faults and as high qual-

ities as are the birthright of any
other in the world." The men were
" true as steel to a friend and beautifully tender and courtly in their
intercourse with women." But this
life was presented not from its own
point of view and with its own tender and hallowed associations, but
from the point of view of an ag-
gressive, vigorous, typical Northerner—one who had served in Sherman's army. Beautiful examples
of practical reconstruction were thus
afforded, and good results followed.
But Judge La Rue, Col. Vance, etc.,
are somewhat conventional. They
are rather types of what the world
has been calling the Southern colonel and the Southern judge. With
" Lucie La Rue " and " Rosalie
Chenier " he has succeeded better.
Rosalie is a pure, sweet child of
Nature who, after the manner of
American women, buds and blos-
soms quickly under suitable conditions into perfect womanhood. But
Lucie is the author's most perfect cre-

ation. With self-possession and self-control, engendered by generations of good breeding, she is artless, genuine, simple, refined. She is worthy to hang in the same portrait gallery with "Aurore" and "Clotilde"—the finest feminine creations the writer has found in contemporary novels. But these are charming stories, among the very best of the many novels of Southern life, and suffused with all the author's accustomed freshness and love of nature. A later and stronger novel is "A Banker at Bankersville"—a vivid, wholesome picture of life in Indiana. The study of the banker was timely, and though this is not a "novel of purpose," it has doubtless served a good purpose. It may have helped to mold the public sentiment which sent a certain banker to the Ohio penitentiary. But what is still better, the author is a practical illustration of his own teaching In a letter to the writer he mentioned a fact worth knowing in the life of a literary man. " I own my own home," says he, "a good and comfortable one, and a landed estate of some value, a good scientific and literary library, a good law library, and am reasonably provided for in every way—all of my own earning, not a cent of it a gift from any person or the result of chance or accident."

"A Fortnight of Folly " (1888) is one of those lapses which imaginative writers are almost sure to make at some time or other in their creative efforts. But, in a series of stories in the *Century*, beginning in 1889, he again becomes natural and interesting. " Two Old Boys " is sheer fun and delightful. Most of these, however, are negro stories, in which the author has attempted to set great political and social truths in a frame of romance with a considerable border of humor and satire. Extremists will find small delight in their teaching, for it is too human and true; but every one may enjoy the genuine humor, blended as it is with a singularly poetic sense of pathos as grotesque as tender. Mr. Thompson's love of a good story doubtless induced him to accept the invitation to write the " Story of Louisiana " (1888). The glamour of romance and the legendary atmosphere belonging to the history of this State must have appealed strongly to "a poet by nature delighting in his poetic theme." There is evident delight in his telling of the dramatic tale of this land abounding in interest of every sort: "landscape, hereditary singularities, mixed nationality, legends, and thrilling episodes." The creole, too, appeals to the author's heart as well as to his imagination, and he puts in an eloquent plea for him. From beginning to end the story is told with spirit, candor, and impartiality, and with unflagging interest to the reader. His latest attempt at story telling, the " Ocala Boy " (1895), is a slight tale for

boys, and while it is not one of the
best specimens either of the author's
skill in narration, or of his ability to
depict life and individual character
(Louis and Rhett are rather too
bookish and "grown up"), it nevertheless has all of his exquisite
charm and freshness in description,
and has the power also of holding
the young reader's delighted attention from beginning to end.

But Mr. Thompson is still more
widely known for his love of nature
and the artistic interpretation of it.
Some of his papers have been collected into two volumes, whose very
titles are refreshing : " Byways and
Bird Notes " (1885), and " Sylvan
Secrets " (1887). Many more are
found in the columns of the *Independent* and other periodical publi-
cations. Almost every article gives
evidence of the enthusiastic naturalist and bird lover. He has tramped
all over the hill country of Florida,
wandering from Tallahassee to Pensacola and Mobile, and on into

Maurice Thompson.

Louisiana, that he might watch and study the mocking bird in its native groves. Equally well known to him are the catbird, thrush, woodpecker, jay, bluebird, kingfisher, heron, and many more of the feathered denizens of wood and stream. Especially in bird studies has he excelled, some of them being so accurate and original as to overthrow the theories of so celebrated a scientist as Mr. Huxley, and to correct the mistakes of so great a lover of birds as Alexander Wilson. But he is an observer of nature from the poetic and literary side too, and this knowledge is communicated to us in so delightful a way that we are often unable to determine which delights us the more, the literary artist or the keen-eyed observer. Thought seems to come to him always under the laws of form and glowing with color. But there is much more in these essays than love of nature and exquisite descriptions. Here we find

124

his methods of study, his theories of
criticism, and a warm human element, which, combined with fre-
quent moralizings as racy and invigorating as his best outdoor studies, show him as he really is, a vigorous thinker and true philosopher,
and a breezy, inspiriting, suggestive
critic. His paper on " Shakespeare" is in the opinion of many
the best essay he has written. Like
his poems on those well - worn
themes of classic allegory, it is instinct with life—fresh, bold, original. His poem on " Diana " and
his paper on " Shakespeare " show
that the true poet and the real thinker can put life and beauty into subjects so old and trite that form and
motion seem no longer possible to
them. These papers take a wide
range. At one time we are in the
" haunts of the mocking bird ;" then
we find ourselves in a " Southern
swamp," " a genuine land of
dreams ; " anon we spend awhile
with Ruskin and Shakespeare by

the gulf, with the sunshine and the
wind of the South flowing over us.

In more recent years the short
literary essay has claimed his chief
attention. It is easy to see that the
love of books has been growing
upon him. Indeed, he has been
seen to neglect grayling and trout for
Theocritus, and his " Pindaric Perspective " is as exhilarating as the
" King of the Brambles." The "Art
of Suggestion " discloses his sympathetic study of the poets, as well
as the rich suggestiveness or wonderful under-meaning so apparent
in them. His treatment of every
subject reveals the fact that here is
one who delights in freshness and
originality, while frankness and
individuality are observable in every
line. He goes beyond æsthetics to
ethics in art, " for life and literature
cannot be separated so as to say
that what is vicious in life is harm-
lessly delectable in literature." His
objection to the nude in art is presented in this way : " Fitness is a

large element of ethics; it is everything in æsthetics. Nude art was
fit in the days when religion was
lasciviousness and civilization's highest aspiration a dream of unspeakable debauchery; man's duty was
not visible to him, and he groveled
after mere animal gratifications.
Nude art, as we see it in the old
sculptures, the old drawings, and
the old poems, expressed with all
the glory of benighted yet divine
genius the actualities of pagan life.
Nakedness was the heathen's spiritual and, in a large degree, physical
condition, while it is ours to be
clothed upon with the garments of
decency. Our ethics cannot escape
the fitness of the Christian fashion;
much less can our æsthetics go back
to pagan modes." For this reason
he abominates realism, because it is
both false and unhealthy. " These
modern realists utter the cry of our
civilization's lowest and most be-
lated element," while "the great
masters of art lift us above the mire

of degrading things." Romance
and heroism he continues to recognize as the two greatest forces in
human life, nor has he got beyond
Homer and Shakespeare and Sir
Walter Scott and Thackeray. He
is specially fond of the Greeks, Theocritus above all, because " freshness hung upon their thoughts like
a dew of morning." In them there
is nothing alien, nothing insincere,
unnatural, unhealthy. But one is
apt to misunderstand Mr. Thompson's writings about the Greeks,
and all poets, unless one remembers
that the poet's and the scholar's
points of view may be, and most
often are, far apart. His view of
criticism is best presented in that excellent little volume, the " Ethics
of Literary Art " (1893), which is
not only healthy, stimulating, suggestive throughout, but is also the
timeliest antidote to the disease-
bearing fiction of the day that has
yet been offered. Of him as a
writer on nature and books we may

say in his own words: "One who
comes to us with the joy of health
in his nerves and the sweets of nature's wild breath upon his lips is an
incarnate blessing. The philosophy
in his soul is the same as that which
hangs a scarf of amethyst on the
mountain; his bodily health is like
the vigor of a plant in spring; his
speech is fragrance."

But Mr. Thompson is above all the
poet. Even his prose is poetic and
imaginative. Though he studies
Nature with the calm dispassionate-
ness of a scientist, he loves her with
the imaginative love of a poet. He
cannot, however, be likened to Spen-
ser,

Who, like a copious river, poured his song
   O'er all the mazes of enchanted ground.

His earlier poems, " Songs of Fair
Weather " (1883), are rather rivulets,
clear, limpid, sparkling, and not seldom little wellsprings of freshness
and gladness bursting from the
depths of nature and the human

Maurice Thompson.

heart. They are all songs of fair weather. Storms and clouds are far away. The cool, fresh, sweet air of early spring blows through them, though now and then there is a breeze wafted across fields of new-mown hay. As Mr. W. D. Howells beautifully said: "The odor of the woods, pure and keen and clean, seems to strike up from this verse as directly as from the mold in the heart of the primeval forest; but it is as exquisite as if thrice distilled in some chemist's alembic, the last effect of his cunning in perfumes." To his own conception of a poet he answers well:

> He is a poet strong and true,
> Who loves wild thyme and honeydew,
> And like a brown bee works and sings;
> With morning freshness on his wings,
> And a gold burden on his thighs—
> The pollendust of centuries.

One of the greatest charms of his poetry is the combination of perfect simplicity of expression with exquisite tenderness of feeling and beauty of thought. There is no straining after effect; there are no archaic words, no feeble imitations of the old poets. His words are simple and homely, yet they express perfectly his ideas. They do more: they carry us into the higher realms of thought, of feeling, and of the imagination. Take this little stanza from one of his best poems, "At My Window," as an example:

A breath from tropical borders,
    Just a ripple flowed into my room,
And washed my face clean of its sadness,
    Blew my heart into bloom.

What suggestiveness there is in the closing stanzas of " November ! "

Calmly I wait the dreary change—
    The season cutting sharp and sheer
Through the wan bowers of death that fringe
    The border of the year.

And while I muse the fated earth
    Into a colder current dips;
Feels winter's scourge with summer's kiss
    Still warm upon her lips.

131

Maurice Thompson.

What could be more delicate and subtle than some of his lines:

The wind drew faintly from the South,
Like breath blown from a sleeper's mouth!

And

Bubble, bubble, flows the stream,
Like an old tune through a dream.

Indeed, in all these poems we feel

The influence, sweet and slight,
Of strange, elusive perfume, blown
Off dewy groves by night.

These songs rank with the very best of their kind, and this ràre little first volume was welcomed as one of the most genuinely poetic contributions to American literature.

In 1892 a new edition of these songs, slightly enlarged, was published under the simple title of "Poems." The newcomers necessitated the change in the title, for to the dewy freshness, spontaneity, and outdoor singing, as natural as a bird's, of the young roamer at will with gun, or bow and arrows, or fishing rod, have been added the more conscious efforts of the matur-

132

er student of books and of men.
There is nothing, however, that
savors of the lamp and the close
room.   But to some extent one feels
that the songs of a mocking bird
are "translated carefully," and that
it is impossible to reproduce the
" golden note by golden word," even
though

> Heard in dewy dawn-lit ways
>   Of Freedom's solitudes
> Down by the sea in the springtime woods.

But in spite of this inability to attain the unattainable, there is many
a beautiful picture, as well as many
a noble thought, framed in the exquisite lines of " In Captivity," " To
an English Nightingale," "To an
English Skylark," and " B e f o r e
Sunrise "—all songs of the mocking
bird.

Again and again in his poems, in
all of his writings, is revealed his
deep and tender love for the South.
His war poems are often resonant,
and long lingering in the mind of

reader or hearer. To the memory of his comrades he sings :

Remembering the boys in gray,
    With thoughts too deep and fine for
        words,
I lift this cup of love to-day
    To drink what only love affords.

But his choicest, heartiest lines are for

    The South whose gaze is cast
    No more upon the past,
But whose bright eyes the skies of prom-
    ise sweep,
Whose feet in paths of progress swiftly
    leap;
And whose fresh thoughts, like cheerful
    rivers run,
Through odorous ways to meet the morn-
    ing sun!

Mr. Thompson's masterpiece, though not his most perfect poem, is " Lincoln's Grave " (1894), a poem read before the Phi Beta Kappa Brotherhood of Harvard College. His ideal of Lincoln is high both in the poetic sense and in the judicial sense of the worth of the man, whose wonderfully kind heart and tender compassion have won for him the

ever increasing affection of the
American people, just as his signal
ability in controlling the destinies of
his country in the hour of its most
agonizing struggle excited the admiration of the world. But it is as
the overlooking, all-pitying, tender
leader of the people that Mr. Thompson presents him most successfully.
He sees him feeling every pain of that
awful time. Possibly the thought is
most fully set out in this stanza:

He was the Southern mother leaning
forth,
At dead of night to hear the cannon
roar,
Beseeching God to turn the cruel North
And break it, that her son might come
once more;
He was New England's maiden, pale and
pure,
Whose gallant lover fell on Shiloh's
plain;
He was the mangled body of the dead;
He writhing did endure
Wounds and disfigurement and racking
pain,
Gangrene and amputation, all things
dread.

Maurice Thompson.

And the true spirit of the great man is best conceived in these lines:

> "No selfish aim
> Guided one thought of all those trying hours;
> No breath of pride,
> No pompous striving for the pose of fame,
> Weakened one stroke of all his noble powers.

In person Mr. Thompson is above medium height, slender, almost slight, but straight, lithe and compact; a sinewy athlete, with a large head, dark-brown eyes, black hair, dark skin, a thin, strongly marked face, semiaquiline nose, and a long, very slight moustache. He is a hard and rapid worker. In the morning, from an early hour to the midday lunch, he works steadily at his desk, which is an old mahogany curiosity mounted in ancient brass and cunningly constructed; and in the afternoon he gives himself up to recreation. He has risen fast, and his influence is strongly marked, especially in the criticism of poetry and fiction.

Sidney Lanier.

O golden legend writ in the skies!
  I turn toward you with longing soul,
And list to the awful harmonies
  Of the spheres as on they roll.

THE bearer of an evangel of truth and beauty to the world may ever expect a tardy acceptance of his mission. " For he is an embodied ideal sent into the world to rebuke its commonplace aims, and to leaven its dull, brute mass," and his rich and fragrant influences are too often shed upon " souls long coffined in indolent conventions." Not unfrequently he is made to sigh with the German poet:

O! for all I have suffered and striven,
  Care has embittered my cup and my
    feast;
But here is the night and the dark-blue
    heaven,
  And my soul shall be at rest.

Sidney Lanier.

For the world deals strangely with
its poets. They come so seldom
and in such ever new and changed
garb that oftentimes only the saving
remnant recognizes their existence.
Sometimes, too, the poet's life is
strangely at variance with his message, and the world satisfies its dull
self-complacency by simply telling
the " truth " about him.

But here is one whose beauty of
personality is no whit inferior to the
loftiness and worth of his message.
He was a spotless, sunny-souled,
hard-working, divinely gifted man,
who had exalted ideas both of art
and of life, and he

Lived and sang that life and song
  Might each express the other's all,
Careless if life or art were long,
  Since both were one, to stand or fall.
So that the wonder struck the crowd,
  Who shouted it about the land;
His song was only living aloud,
  His work a singing with his hand.

But the shout was raised after he
was called away. During his life-

time he was left to the accumulated ills of poverty, neglect, disease, and premature death. " Better late than never " is a good old adage, and it is well to consider that Sidney Lanier is already generally recognized as the most distinctive figure in our literature since the famous group of New England poets passed away, and that many are already claiming for him the right to rank among the few genuine poets of America.

The story of his personality and work, though pathetic, is one of the most interesting and inspiring in the biographical annals of men of letters. Sidney Lanier sprang from a Huguenot family, the founder of which, on English soil, was Jerome Lanier, who emigrated with his family to England in the latter part of the reign of Queen Elizabeth and obtained employment in her household service. It is probable that he was a musical composer and shared in the production of those

musical dramas and masques which
"so did take Eliza and our James."
Between the years 1568 and 1666
ten Laniers flourished in England,
enjoying the favor of four consecu-
tive English monarchs.

Nicholas Lanier, son of Jerome,
received, as painter, engraver, "master of the king's music," and diplo-
matist, the encouragement of James
I. and the friendship of Charles I.
During the reign of James I. he set
to music two of Ben Jonson's
masques, "The Vision of Delight,"
and the " Masque of Lethe ; " and in
the time of Charles I. his name is
associated with that of Henry Lawes,
the composer of the songs for Milton's "Comus." This Nicholas was
a friend of Van Dyck, who painted
his portrait. His son, also named
Nicholas, was much in favor with
Charles II. He too was a lover of
pictures, as was his father and an
Uncle Jerome, who had a fine collection at Greenwich, the home of

the Laniers for several generations.
But he was still more interested in
music, and, uniting with a number
of other persons, including four ad-
ditional Laniers, he obtained the re-
newal of a charter for the Society
of Musicians, in which he was ap-
pointed First Marshal or President
for life, with the determination to
"exert their authority for the improvement of the science and the interest of its professors." One of
the other four was John Lanier,
very likely father of the Sir John
Lanier who fought as major general
at the battle of the Boyne, and fell
gloriously at Steinkirk, along with
the brave Douglas.

The first Lanier to come to America was Thomas, in 1716, who settled with other colonists on a grant
of land ten miles square, which included the site of the present city
of Richmond, Va. A descendant
of his by the same name married an
aunt of George Washington, and

the family furnished many honored citizens to the colony and the state. "Again and again the strain of artist's blood has shown itself among them." At present the name is very common in the South.

It is not stated when Sidney's grandfather moved to Georgia, but his father, Mr. Robert S. Lanier, was born there, and after receiving a fair education at a manual labor school, and later at Randolph-Macon College, in Virginia, he became a lawyer, married Miss Mary J. Anderson, of Virginia, whose family supplied members of the House of Burgesses in more than one generation and was gifted in poetry, music, and oratory, and returned to his native state to begin the practice of his profession. He possessed a taste for reading, and accumulated miscellaneous books faster than clients. But his wife's Scotch thrift and his own industry enabled them to live comfortably, if narrowly.

Their first child was born February 3, 1842, on High Street, in Macon, Ga., and named Sidney. Another son, Clifford, and a daughter completed the number. The house stands now nearly as then, on a commanding ridge from which the ground falls rapidly away in three directions, affording many picturesque views from its windows. Near by were happy hunting grounds where the two brothers— loving and inseparable companions from childhood — sought hickory nuts, scaly barks, and haw apples, or hunted doves, blackbirds, robins, plover, snipe, squirrels, and rabbits, according to season and inclination. In such excursions, though Sidney's tastes often pronounced in favor of quiet angling for fish in the placid Ocmulgee, he doubtless imbibed the Wordsworthian love of natural things which has found intense expression in many of his latest poems.

143

His fondness for reading showed itself early, and much of his play-time was spent in the office of his father, adjoining the house, where the family library was kept. But, even at this early age, his passion was music. When he was only a few years old Santa Claus brought him a small, yellow, one-keyed, flageoletlike flute, on which simple instrument he would practice with the passion of a *virtuoso*. Still earlier he had displayed aptitude for music by beating on the bones (such as negro minstrels use) jigs, strath-speys, and dance tunes in accompaniment to the piano playing of his mother. He never received any musical instruction beyond the teaching of the notes to him by his mother, yet at an early age he could play on almost any instrument— flute, piano, guitar, banjo, violin, organ, etc. He says in a letter: " I could play passably well on several instruments before I could write

legibly, and since then the very
deepest of my life has been filled
with music." At this time his boyish delight found expression either
as leader of a children's amateur
minstrel band, or, a little later, as
captain of a boys' military company,
armed with bows and arrows, a result of " Froissart " and " Chronicles
of the English Bowmen." But his
first impulse was ever to form an
amateur orchestra of children, of
schoolboys, of fellow-soldiers in
camp, and he finally became first
flutist of the Peabody Orchestra in
Baltimore.

In disposition and character, as in
gifts and aptitudes, the child was
also father to the man. His high-
spirited fearlessness was admirably
tempered with amiability and a kind
of chivalry, even for one so young,
and his little friends (he always exhibited a special capacity for friendship) were somehow impressed with
his distinction, or, at any rate, with

145

a feeling of his original personality.

The year before he entered college it was deemed best to give him a " taste " of business, and for about a year he was general delivery clerk in the Macon post office. From a boy he had a deep sense of humor and a keen eye for character, and this situation afforded a fine opportunity for their natural growth and enlargement. At the supper table he would keep the family in a roar by mimicry of the funny speech of the Middle Georgia Crackers, the country people applying for letters. Later in his writings, " Tiger Lilies," " Florida," and more particularly in his dialect poems, " Jones of Jones," Jones's Private Argyment," " Civil (or Oncivil) Rights," etc., he gave abundant evidence that he had utilized both observation and experience sufficiently to take rank with the best dialect writers and " character " delineators, if his mind

146

had not been on higher thoughts intent. A genuine humor crops out here and there in his writings, though they were seldom of a humorous kind, and he was always brimful of fun, even when the battle was against him, as the following little pleasantry, acknowledging delicacies sent to his sickbed. will indicate :

How oft the answers to our passing
    prayers
  Drop down in forms our fancy ne'er
    foretold!
Thus when, of late, consumed by wast-
    ing cares,
  "Angels, preserve us!" from my lips
    unrolled,
I'm sure I pictured not, while thus I
    prayed,
Angels, preserve me, would, with *marma-
    lade.*

No account of his school days, except the Saturdays, has yet been given; but he must have had fairly good teachers and instruction, for at a little less than fifteen years of age he was admitted

147

to Oglethorpe College, a small institution under Presbyterian control at Midway, near Milledgeville, which was then the capital of the state. January 6, 1857, he writes home : "We were admitted into our classes, I into "Soph," Will into Junior. I have just done studying to-night my first lesson—to wit, forty-five lines of Horace, which I 'did' in about fifteen minutes." Only one of his teachers seems to have left his impress upon him, Prof. James Woodrow, since widely known as a strong and stimulating professor in the theological seminary at Columbia, S. C., and as President of South Carolina College. To him, as in the last weeks of his life Mr. Lanier stated, he was indebted for the strongest and most valuable stimulus of his life. And in more ways than one did this little college prove to be congenial soil for the development of this rich and luxuriant nature, which, sending

Sidney Lanier.

out its tendrils in every direction,
grew and thrived. He lived in an
atmosphere of ardent and loyal
friendship. His warm and enthusiastic heart and his keenly alert and
capacious mind both demanded fellowship; and already revelations
were gradually coming to him, intimations of what he might learn
from study of books, from art, from
nature, from men. His classmate
and roommate in the Junior year,
Mr. T. F. Newell, vividly describes
this period: "I can recall my
association with him with sweetest pleasure, especially those Attic
nights, for they are among the dearest and tenderest recollections of
my life, when with a few chosen
companions we would read from
some treasured volume, it may have
been Tennyson or Carlyle or Christopher North's "Noctes Ambro-
sianæ," or we would make the hours
vocal with music and song; those
happy nights, which were veritable

149

refections of the gods, and which
will be remembered with no other
regret than that they will never
more return. On such occasions I
have seen him walk up and down
the room and with his flute extem-
porize the sweetest music ever vouch-
safed to mortal ear. At such times
it would seem as if his soul were in
a trance, and could only find existence, expression, in the ecstacy of
tone, that would catch our souls with
his into the very seventh heaven of
harmony. Or in merry mood, I
have seen him take a banjo, for he
could play on any instrument, and
as with deft fingers he would strike
some strange new note or chord, you
would see his eyes brighten, he
would begin to smile and laugh as
if his very soul were tickled, while
his hearers would catch the inspiration, and an old-fashioned ' walk-
round ' and ' negro breakdown,' in
which all would participate, would
be the inevitable result. At other

150

times, with our musical instruments, we would sally forth into the night and 'neath moon and stars and under ' Bonny Bell window panes '—ah, those serenades! were there ever or will there ever be anything like them again?—when the velvet flute notes of Lanier would fall pleasantly upon the night, and

> The bosom of that harmony,
>   And sailed and sailed incessantly,
> As if a petal from a wild rose blown
> Had fluttered down that pool of tone,
> And floated down the glassy tide,
> And clarified and glorified,
> The solemn spaces where shadows bide.

And then on Saturdays we would walk through the groves and the ' gospeling glooms ' of the woods, where every sound was a joy and inspiration. I have never seen one who enjoyed nature more than he. And his love for her was so intense that I have sometimes imagined he could hear the murmur, the music, that springs from the growing of grass.

All tree-sounds, rustling of pine cones,
Wind sighings, doves' melodious moans,
And night's unearthly undertones."

More than once at this period do
we hear of this trance state while he
was playing. Apparently unconscious, he would seem to hear the
richest music; or again he would
awake from a deep trance, alone,
on the floor of his room, and the
nervous strain would leave him sadly shaken in nerves. For this reason his father prevailed upon him
to devote himself to the flute rather
than to the violin, for it was the
violin voice that above all others
commanded his soul. In after
years more than one listener remarked the strange violin effects
which he conquered from the flute.

As a student at college he gave
his spare time chiefly to musical
practice and to reading. He had
earlier read Scott, Froissart, " Gil
Blas," Mayne Reid, " Don Quix-
ote," " Reynard the Fox," and per-

haps some of the eighteenth century English writers. But now he roamed at will in a wider field, and took his delight in Shakespeare, Landor, Keats, Shelley, Coleridge, Schiller, Carlyle, Tennyson, etc. " There was one thing remarkable about Lanier as a student at college," adds Mr. Newell : "Although passionately fond of music, both in theory and in practice, even at that early age conceded by all who had the pleasure of hearing him as the finest of flute players ; although he was ever ready to show his love for nature and art in their various forms and manifestations, yet he was a persistent student, an omnivorous reader of books, and in his college classes was easily first in mathematics as well as in his other studies. He loved all the sciences. The purest fountains of Greek and Roman literature had nourished and fed his youthful mind. But even at that early age I recall how he delighted in the quaint and curious of our old literature. I remember that it was he who introduced me to that rare old book, Burton's 'Anatomy of Melancholy,' whose name and size had frightened me as I first saw it on the shelves, but which I found to be wholly different from what its title would indicate; and old Jeremy Taylor, 'the poet - preacher;' and Keats's 'Endymion' and 'Chatterton,' the 'marvelous boy who perished in his pride.' Yes, I first learned the story of the Monk Rowley and his wonderful poems with Lanier. And Shelley and Coleridge and Christopher North, and that strange, weird poem of 'The Ettrick Shepherd' of 'How Kilmeny Came Hame,' and a whole sweet host and noble company, 'rare and complete.' Yes, Tennyson, with his 'Locksley Hall' and his 'In Memoriam' and his 'Maud,' which last we almost knew by heart. And then old Carlyle with his 'Sartor

Resartus,' ' Hero Worship,' 'Past
and Present,' and his wonderful
book of essays, especially the ones
on Burns and Jean Paul, ' The
Only.' Without a doubt it was
Carlyle who first enkindled in Lanier a love of German literature
and a desire to know more of the
language."

Thus the happy, golden time sped
till he reached graduation, a little
beyond eighteen. With a fellow-
senior he shared the honors of the
day and delivered his essay, entitled " The Philosophy of History,"
which began with a quotation from
Walter Savage Landor, whose writings he admired. He was immediately elected tutor, and returned
in the fall to give only six months,
as it happened, to his new vocation.
But in that short time he did much
miscellaneous reading, and began to
jot down some hints and fragments
of a poetical, musical conception,
which seems to have haunted his

short after life, clamoring for an embodiment which was ever denied it—a sort of musical drama of the peasant uprising in France, called the "Jacquerie." That which did take shape, a mere fragment, and three songs written for it are included in his "Unrevised Early Poems." "These very first poetical efforts linger in my memory," says his brother Clifford, "as being *Byronesque*, if not *Wertheresque*, at least tinged with gloominess as of Young's 'Night [or a young man's nightlike] Thoughts.' . . . He has not preserved any of these lucubrations, perhaps because they were not hale, hearty, breathing of sanity, hope, betterment, aspiration. . . . I have his first attempt at poetry. It is characteristic, it is not suggestive of swallow flights of song, but of an eaglet peering up toward the empyrean."

At the early age of eighteen the pure, high-souled youth confides his thoughts to a notebook which now

affords many attractive glimpses of
his inner life, his aspirations, his
longings, and his keenly alive personality, with its eager outlook upon
and vivid realization of life, its quick
apprehension, its intensity of spirit.
Goethe's wonderful saying, "im
Ganzen, Guten, Wahren resolut zu
leben," might have been adopted as
his motto. And his mind is already
aglow with the thought of writing
something which the world will not
willingly let die, while at the same
time he is more consciously aware
of the divine gift of music in his
soul. "Is it genius?" he asks, all
a-tremble, and begins a memorable
twenty-year struggle with earnest,
humble questionings as to God's will
concerning the use of it. In discussing with himself how far inclinations were to be regarded as indications of capacity and duty, he
says: "The point which I wish to
settle is merely by what method
shall I ascertain what I am fit for,

as preliminary to ascertaining God's
will with reference to me; or what
my inclinations are, as preliminary
to ascertaining what my capacities
are—that is, what I am fit for. I
am more than all perplexed by this
fact: that the prime inclination—that
is, natural bent (which I have
checked, though)—of my nature is to
music, and for that I have the greatest talent; indeed, not boasting, for
God gave it me, I have an extraordinary musical talent, and feel it
within me plainly that I could rise as
high as any composer. But I cannot bring myself to believe that I
was intended for a musician, because
it seems so small a business in comparison with other things which, it
seems to me, I might do. Question
here: ‘What is the province of music in the economy of the world?’”

There is a feeling of inexpressible
sadness on finding this young swan
among the ducklings, for music is no
part of their nature. Nay, more: the

people among whom he was born and lived, including his own father, held it unmanly to be a musician. But young Lanier does not rest content till he finds an answer, at least for himself, to his own question, which he gives only a very few years later in " Tiger Lilies : "

"I wonder how it is that many good American people even now consider music a romantic amusement rather than a common necessity of life! when surely of all the commonplaces none is more broadly common or more inseparable from daily life. Music! It is as common . . . as bricks, common as anvils, common as water, common as fireplaces! For every brick mason sings to his trowel strokes, and blacksmiths strike true rhythmical time, even to triplets—I've heard 'em—and sailors whistle in calm or windy weather, and households jangle and thrum and strain on all manner of stringed and wind instruments. Music is in common life what heat is in chemistry, an all-pervading, ever-present, mysterious genius. The carpenter whistles to cheer his work, the loafer whistles to cheer his idleness. The church for life, and the barroom for death; the theater for tears, and the circus for smiles; the parlor for wealth, and the street for poverty—each of these nowadays has its inevitable, peculiar orchestra. And so every emotion continually calls, like the clown in the play : 'Music without there!' Victory chants, defeat wails; joy has galops, sorrow her dirges; patriotism shouts its *Marseillaise*, and love lives on music for food, says Old Will. Moreover, the Chinese beats his gong, and the African his jawbone; the Greek blew Dorian flutes; the Oriental charms serpents with his flageolet; German Mendelssohn sends up saintly thanks; Polish Chopin pleads for a man's broken heart, and American

Gottschalk fills the room full of great, sad-eyed ghosts—all with the piano! Aye,

> There's not a star that thou beholdest there
> But in his motion like an angel *sings,*
> Still choiring to the young-eyed cherubim!

And so from 'street mud' up to 'star fire," through all grades, runs the multitudinous song of time. From a christening to a funeral is seventy years: one choir sings at the christening, another choir sings at the funeral. All the life between the dead man sang, in some sort, what tunes his heart could make. Late explorers say that they have found some nations that had no God, but I have not read of any that had no music! Wherefore, since in all holy worship, in all unholy sarcasm, in all conditions of life, in all domestic, social, religious, political, and lonely individual doings; in all passions, in all countries, earthly or

heavenly; in all stages of civilization, of time, or of eternity; since, I
say, in all these music is always
present to utter the shallowest or
the deepest thoughts of man or
spirit—let us cease to call music a
fine art, to class it with delicate
pastry cookery and confectionery, and
to fear to take too much of it lest it
should make us sick!"

Again he writes: "I wish that in
all the colleges [here in the South]
the professor of music were considered, as he should be, one of the
professors of metaphysics, and that
he ranked of equal dignity with
them, and that he stood as much
chance of being elected President of
the college as the professor of chemistry or the languages." These ex-
tracts show how the artist in him
was cabined, cribbed, confined, and
bound in to a life which offered no
stimulus to the cultivation of his
gift, and but scanty appreciation of
or sympathy with it, and that, too,

when he is conscious of the fact that,
as he wrote to a friend as late as
1873, "whatever turn I may have
for art is purely *musical*, poetry being with me *a mere tangent* into
which I shoot sometimes."

But only six months were given
to these questionings, when a more
practical struggle claimed his attention. "The early spring of 1861
brought to bloom, besides innumerable violets and jessamines, a strange,
enormous, and terrible flower. This
was the blood-red flower of war,
which grows amid thunders; a
flower whose freshening dews are
blood and hot tears, whose shadow
chills a land, whose odors strangle a
people, whose giant petals droop
downward, and whose roots are in
hell. It is a species of the great
genus, sin flower, which is so conspicuous in the flora of all ages and
all countries, and whose multifarious
leafage and fruitage so far overgrow
a land that the violet, or love genus,

has often small chance to show its quiet blue." So experience taught the man to think; but a certain military taste, early shown in the boyish ardor for bows and arrows, drills, and military parades, and a well-nigh universal war fever which attacked the Southern people, swept the young tutor and his still younger brother into the Macon Volunteers and the Second Georgia Battalion and on to the bloody battlefields of Virginia. They entered as privates, and both, though offered promotion —Sidney three times—remained privates, so singularly tender was their devotion to each other.

During the first year, spent amid the delights of Norfolk society and the Norfolk market, his service was light. But this Capua was soon exchanged for the marches and hardships incident to the battles of Seven Pines, Drewry's Bluffs, and the seven days' fighting around Richmond, culminating in the terrible

164

struggle of Malvern Hill, in all of which he took part. He was then transferred to the signal service, and for a short period his headquarters were at Petersburg, where he had the advantage of a small local library. Later he was detached for outpost duty as a mounted signal scout.

After describing a skirmish at Fort Boykin in 1863 his brother adds: " Nearly two years were passed in such skirmishes, racing to escape the enemy's gunboats, signaling dispatches, serenading country beauties, poring over chance books, and foraging for provender along the Blackwater." His conduct throughout was marked by a strict adherence to discipline as well as the bright *insouciance* of the American citizen-soldier ; but neither pleasure nor hardships could win him from music and study, or veil from his eyes the beauties of nature. In camp he tries to set some of

Tennyson's songs to music, especially one in Elaine, "The Song of
Love and Death." He studies the
German language, and translates in
intervals of repose or at night, after
his horse is curried, Heine, Goethe,
and Schiller for self-instruction.
While he is serving with a detach-
ment of scouts the enemy surprises
their little camp and carries off, besides their clothes, cooking utensils,
and cots, his treasures—"Heine,"
"Aurora Leigh," "Les Miserables,"
"Macaria," and a German glossary.
But no one but a poet could capture
the glassy, cool, transculent wave of
Burwell's Bay, the white shell beach,
mile upon mile, the towering bluff
decked with a million green mosses
and trickling springs and crowned
with great oaks holding out their
arms from the top in a perpetual
attitude of blessing, and the vast expanse across Hampton Roads, out
between the capes, on to the broad
waters. No, nor that little garden

166

of Eden there, now hid away in
"Tiger Lilies" — "a small dell
which is round as a basin, two hundred yards in diameter, shut in on
all sides. Beeches, oaks, lithe hick-
ories, straight pines, roof over this
dell with a magnificent boscage. In
the center of it bubbles a limpid
spring. Shy companies of flowers
stand between the long grasses;
some of them show wide, startled
eyes, many of them have hidden
away in cunning nooks. Over
them, regarding them in silent and
passionate tenderness, lean the eb-
ony-fibered ferns; and the busy
mosses do their very best to hide
all rudeness and all decay behind a
green velvet arras. The light does
not dare shine very brightly here;
it is soft and sacred, tempered with
green leaves, with silence, with
odors, with beauties. Wandering
perfumes, restless with happiness,
float about aimlessly; they are the
only inhabitants here." Amid these

scenes there was a renewed " stirring
within his soul of that genius which
was to place him among that good-
ly company whose fellowship he so
dearly loved." One who knew him
at this time describes him as a slender, gray-eyed youth, full of enthusiasm, playful with a dainty
mirthfulness, a tender humor, most
like the great musician, Mendelssohn.

In 1864 the brothers were separated, Sidney being assigned to
duty as signal officer to the blockade runner "Annie." On the first
run out of East Inlet, near Fort
Fisher, she was captured, and Sidney, refusing to don the clothes of
his fellow-officers, Englishmen, and
declare himself a foreigner, was
taken to Point Lookout prison,
" where were sown the seeds of
fell disease, to retard whose growth
was the greatest part of his endeav-
or for the following few years."
These days of confinement were

cheered by fellowship with a kindred spirit, another prisoner since widely known as the poet-priest, Father Tabb, and solaced by his inseparable companion through life, his flute, which he had carried hidden in his sleeve into the prison with him. After five months he was released on an exchange of prisoners, but owing to his thin clothing and the cold weather he came near dying on the water voyage to City Point. The story of his rescue from death is graphically told by the lady herself who was the good Samaritan on this occasion. She was an old friend from Montgomery, Ala., returning from New York to Richmond; and her little daughter, who had learned to call him "Brother Sid," chanced to hear that he was down in the hold of the vessel dying. On application to the colonel in command permission was promptly given to her to minister to his necessity, and she made haste to go below. "Now my friends in New York," continued she, "had given me a supply of medicines, for we had few such things in Dixie, and among the remedies were quinine and brandy. I hastily took a flask of brandy, and we went below, where we were led to the rude stalls provided for cattle, but now crowded with poor human wretches. There in that horrible place dear Sidney Lanier lay wrapped in an old quilt, his thin hands tightly clinched, his face drawn and pinched, his eyes fixed and staring, his poor body shivering now and then in a spasm of pain. Lilla fell at his side, kissing him and calling: 'Brother Sid, don't you know me? Don't you know your little sister?' But no recognition or response came from the sunken eyes. I poured some brandy into a spoon and gave it to him. It gurgled down his throat at first with no effort from him to

170

swallow it. I repeated the stimulant several times before he finally revived. At last he turned his eyes slowly about until he saw Lilla, and murmured: 'Am I dead? Is this Lilla? Is this heaven?' . . . To make a long story short, the colonel assisted us to get him above to our cabin. I can see his fellow-prisoners now as they crouched and assisted to pass him along over their heads, for they were so packed that they could not make room to carry him through. Along over their heads they tenderly passed the poor, emaciated body, so shrunken with prison life and benumbed with cold. We got him into clean blankets, but at first he could not endure the pain from the fire, he was so nearly frozen. We gave him some hot soup and more brandy, and he lay quiet till after midnight. Then he asked for his flute and began playing. As he played the first few notes, you should have heard the yell of joy that came up from the shivering wretches down below, who knew that their comrade was alive. And there we sat entranced about him, the colonel and his wife, Lilla and I, weeping at the tender music, as the tones of new warmth and color and hope came like liquid melody from his magic flute."

In this enfeebled condition he was landed in February, 1865, and as soon as the exchange was effected he set out on foot for his far-away Georgia home. A twenty-dollar gold piece, which he had in his pocket when captured—doubtless the small sum kept by him when the English captain of the "Annie," just before capture, directed him to distribute the ship's money among the crew, and an old tar having been overlooked, Lanier gave him all his share but this—and which was returned to him when released—and the friend-making, comfort-earning flute were his sole possessions. Weary and footsore, he plodded along till March 15, when he reached home utterly exhausted in strength. The hardships of camp and prison life, the bitter cold at sea, and the long, weary journey had proved too much for his constitution, and six weeks of desperate illness was the result. The first days of his recovery witnessed the death of his mother from consumption, and he himself arose from his sick bed with pronounced congestion of one lung. Such, however was the elasticity of his nature —a quality for which he was ever remarkable—that two months with an uncle at Point Clear, on Mobile Bay, where he lived for the most part out of doors and breathed the invigorating, life-giving air of pines and of sea, brought the necessary relief.

Later in life Mr. Lanier wrote to Bayard Taylor: "Perhaps you know that with us of the younger generation in the South, since the war, pretty much the whole of life has been merely not dying." Doubtless he had in mind the years of his life between 1865 and 1873. In September, 1865, he writes, amid the uncongenial atmosphere of the schoolroom in a private family : " I'm busy with brain since I wrote you. . . . Have little leisure. . . . Thirty classes a day . . . and failing health prevents sitting up late at night. It almost maddens me to be confined to the horrible monotony of tare and tret (it should be swear and fret) when my brain is fairly teeming with beautiful things."

In December of the same year this servitude was exchanged for a clerkship in a hotel in Montgomery, Ala., whose prosaic duties he discharged till April, 1867, when, having brought to completion his first book, a novel entitled " Tiger Lilies," he made, the following month, his first visit to New York City in search of

174

a publisher. In regard to the time taken to write this volume various incorrect statements have been published—all doubtless due to incorrect information. One says, " written in April; " another states that " he wrote in six weeks his only novel," and still another speaks of it as "a novel written within three weeks and published immediately thereafter." In a letter to the writer, received October 9, 1896, Mrs. Lanier writes : " Very recently I have seen a letter of 1867, written to his father while he was finishing the manuscript that had begun its growth in 1862 or 1863 in the atmosphere of camp life. He says of it that, having been written at intervals during several years, it reads like a book that was begun by a boy and was finished by a man, and that he intended to leave it so, as an interesting study of literary growth." In regard to the repeated inquiry why she does not have " Tiger

Lilies" republished—it is now out of print, and rare copies bring a good sum—Mrs. Lanier says: "There are portions of it that ought to be preserved, I am sure; but in addition to feeling an inequality that is much to the disadvantage of the opening chapters—chapters that are largely discursive moods of a soldier lad whose chaos has not yet taken shape—I am restrained by a passing remark of the author's, made in August, 1881, when words were very few. The book must have been alluded to, for I recall the thoughtful, half-tender tone when he said: 'Perhaps we will rewrite "Tiger Lilies" some day.' I have always accepted this as a definite assurance that he did not wish to reprint the book as it stood." The letter of 1867, however, "seems to make almost a reason for keeping the work alive as it stands."

Mr. Clifford Lanier, in a private letter of September 21, 1896, says:

"Please remember that the artist in Sidney Lanier would have suppressed so crude and boyish an essay. It is merely a curiosity. It is a welter of suggestions tossing in the mind of a young man passing through the 'sturm und drang" period. It is eccentric as a meteoric sky in August. It is a mesh of roots from which perfect flowers grew. Some of it was conceived, if not written, during military scout duty in Virginia. It is not thought out, but poured out, like the lead fused in a ladle for bullets by a hunter. It is a phantasmagoria of one who wakes from the nightmare of the Civil War."

Few first books could be resurrected with so little drawback to the author's reputation. Its chief value is in the light thrown on the mind and character of the author, and no student of the life and writings of Sidney Lanier can afford to neglect this volume. His voice is just

changing from boy's to man's, now
an airy treble; anon, a gruff bass.
The tender strain of "Hyperion"
suddenly jars into the savage growl
of "Sartor Resartus." Here is a
touch of Vergil or Chopin; there, of
Shakespeare or Beethoven. "He
scatters thoughts as a wind shakes
dewdrops f r o m a bourgeoning
spray"—a poet's thoughts and a
poet's fancies of God and earth and
nature and friends and home and
books and music—and war, too, and
his experiences in prison. But the
ever recurring theme is m u s i c.
Now it is the flute, with which the
musicale should always begin. "It
is like walking in the woods, among
wild flowers, just before you go into
some vast cathedral. For the flute
seems to me to be peculiarly the
woods instrument; it speaks the
gloss of green leaves or the pathos
of bare branches; it calls up the
strange mosses that are under dead
leaves; it breathes of wild plants
178

that hide and oak fragrances that vanish; it expresses to me the natural magic of music." Again it is an accompaniment that " did not follow, but went with the voice, waving and floating and wreathing around the voice like an airy robe around a sweet, flying form above us."

His idea of making a home out of a household is : " Given the raw materials—to wit, wife, children, a friend or two, and a house—two other things are necessary. These are a good fire and good music. And inasmuch as we can do without the fire for half the year, I may say that music is the one essential. After the evening spent around the piano, or the flute, or the violin, how warm and how chastened is the kiss with which the family all say good-night! Ah, the music has taken all the day cares and thrown them into its terrible alembic, and boiled them and rocked them and cooled them till they are crystallized into one

179

care, which is a most sweet and rare desirable sorrow—the yearning for God. We all, from little toddler to father, go to bed with so much of heaven in our hearts, at least, as that we long for it unutterably, and believe it." And still again his description of the violin—one could quote indefinitely his imaginative and picturesque words descriptive of men or moods or trees or scenes, very fanciful at times, but always resplendent with truth and beauty.

This is indeed a "luxuriant, unpruned, but promising" work, and we cannot but regret the necessity of his being compelled to return to the old life again, with its teaching, business, and law, its skirmishes of bread winning against soul expressing, its battles of disease against health. But in September, 1867, he was again in the schoolroom in charge of an academy with nearly a hundred pupils at Prattville, Ala., where he remained one year.

Sidney Lanier.

In the meantime a new inspiration and vital force entered into his life, bringing that abiding faith and stimulating hope to the poet, and congenial companionship and true conjugal love to the man, which only a rarely gifted, perfect help-meet can impart. He was married December 19 to Miss Mary Day, daughter of Charles Day, of Macon, Ga. Now could he sing:

Twice-eyed, with thy gray vision set in
    mine,
  I ken far lands to wifeless men un-
    known;
I compass stars for one-sexed eyes too
    fine.

For her part was to give not only everyday helpfulness and sustaining courage, but also suggestiveness and inspiration—all of which the poet recognizes in " My Springs : "

In the heart of the hills of life I know
Two springs that with unbroken flow
Forever pour their lucent streams
Into my soul's fair Lake of Dreams.
.   .   .   .

Sidney Lanier.

Always when faith with stifling stress
Of grief hath died in bitterness,
I gaze in my two springs and see
A faith that smiles immortally.

Always, when art, on perverse wing,
Flies where I cannot hear him·sing,
I gaze in my two springs and see
A charm that brings him back to me.
. . . .

O Love, O Wife, thine eyes are they,
My Springs, from out whose shining gray
Issue the sweet celestial streams
That feed my life's bright Lake of
    Dreams.

Oval and large and passion pure
And gray and wise and honor sure,
Soft as a dying violet breath,
Yet calmly unafraid of death.
. . . .

Dear eyes, dear eyes! and rare complete—
Being heavenly sweet and earthly sweet—
I marvel that God made you mine,
For when he frowns, 'tis then ye shine!

In January, 1868, came the first
hemorrhage, and in May he returned to Macon low in health, but
determined to study and practice
law with his father as soon as he
should sufficiently recuperate. He

182

seemed to have a presentiment that
such would be his fate, for in
"Tiger Lilies" he says: "Of
course John Sterling studied law—
what young man in our part of the
country did not?" And then he
adds, "John Sterling, Jr., went
forth and committed what may
most properly be called a chrono-
logical error. He took a wife
before he took any fees—surely a
grand mistake in point of time,
where the fees are essentially necessary to get bread for the wife!
Nor was it long before this mistake
made itself apparent. Two extra
mouths, of little Philip and Felix
Sterling, with that horrid propensity
to be filled which mouths will exhibit spite of education and the
spiritual in man, appeared in his
household; outgo began to exceed
income; clouds came to obscure the
financial sky. Even to those of us
who are born to labor, and know it,
it is yet a pathetic sight to see a

man like John Sterling going to his
office every morning to sit there all
day face to face with the 'horny-
eyed phantom' of unceasing drudgery that has no visible end ; to know
that every hour this man will have
some fine yearning beat back in his
face by the Heenan fists in this big
prize ring we call the world, wherein it would seem that toughness of
nose-muscle and active dodging do
most frequently come out with the
purse and the glory."

It is curious that this should have
been published before his marriage,
but he could not have more perfectly represented the situation in which
he now found himself. His health
too grew worse, though fitfully, and
in the summer and spring of 1870
there was a marked decline, with
settled cough. This took him to
New York for treatment, and after
two months he returned much im-
proved as he thought, but in reality
there was the same steady decline.

Sidney Lanier.

By December, 1872, he had given up hope of permanent relief in his Georgia home and gone to San Antonio, Tex., in search of a new home, leaving wife and children behind. But the soft healing air of this region could bring no relief to one whose whole being was hungering and thirsting to express itself in music and poetry. To his wife he writes:

Were it not for some circumstances which make such a proposition seem absurd in the highest degree, I would think that I am shortly to die, and that my spirit hath been singing its swan song before dissolution. All day my soul hath been cutting swiftly into the great space of the subtle, unspeakable deep, driven by wind after wind of heavenly melody. The very inner spirit of and essence of all wind songs, bird songs, passion songs, folk songs, country songs, sex songs, soul songs, and body songs hath blown upon me in quick gusts like the breath of passion, and sailed me into a sea of vast dreams, whereof each wave is at once a vision and a melody.

And so in April, 1873, he returned
185

with the conviction ever becoming
deeper that he had but a short time
in which to do his life work, and
that life work was to be not in law,
but in music and letters.

We catch a glimpse of the inner
struggles, which went on during
these years, in his first letter to
Bayard Taylor, August 17, 1875:
" I could never describe to you what
a mere drought and famine my life
has been as regards that multitude
of matters which I fancy one absorbs when one is in an atmosphere
of art, or when one is in conversa-
tional relation with men of letters,
with travelers, with persons who
have either seen, or written, or done
large things." Step by step he was
driven to follow his natural bent, to
seek a musical atmosphere and a
land of books and the companionship of those who could understand
his longings and appreciate his gifts·

From Baltimore, November 29,
1873, he writes to his father, who

generously offers him a share in his
business and income :

My dear father, think how, for twenty
years, through poverty, through pain,
through weariness, through sickness,
through the uncongenial atmosphere of
a farcical college, and a bare army, and
then of an exacting business life, through
all the discouragement of being wholly
unacquainted with literary people and literary ways—I say, think how, in spite of
all these depressing circumstances, and of
a thousand more which I could enumer-
ate, these two figures of music and of
poetry have steadily kept in my heart so
that I could not banish them. Does it
not seem to you, as to me, that I begin to
have the right to enroll myself among
the devotees of these two sublime arts,
after having followed them so long and
so humbly, and through so much bitterness?

After another visit to New York he
made his home in Baltimore, beginning in December, 1873, an engage-
ment as first flute for the Peabody
Symphony Concerts. In the spring
of 1874 he writes : " I've shed all
the tears about it that I'm going to,

and am now pumping myself full of
music and poetry, with which I pro-
pose to water the dry world. . . .
God has cut me off inexorably from
any other life than this (literary and
artistic). So, St. Cecilia to the rescue! and I hope *God* will like my
music."

To Paul H. Hayne, whom he had
never seen, but with whom he had
exchanged many a pleasant letter,
he writes in May:

I spent last winter in Baltimore, pursuing music and meditating my "Jacquerie." I was *flauto-primo* of the Peabody Symphony Orchestra, and God only
could express the delight and exultation
with which I helped to perform the great
works brought out by that organization
during the season. Of course this was a
queer place for me. Aside from the complete *bouleversement* of proceeding from
the courthouse to the footlights, I was a
raw player and a provincial withal, without practice, and guiltless of instruction--
for I had never had a teacher. To go
under these circumstances among old
professional players, and assume a lead·

ing part in a large orchestra which was organized expressly to play the most difficult works of the great masters, was (now that it's all over) a piece of temerity that I don't remember ever to have equaled before. But I trusted in love, pure and simple, and was not disappointed; for, as if by miracle, difficulties and discouragements melted away before the fire of a passion for music which grows ever stronger within my heart; and I came out with results more gratifying than it is becoming in me to specify. 'Tis quite settled that I cannot practice law. Either writing or speaking appears to produce small hemorrhages which completely sap my strength; and I am going in a few weeks to New York, without knowing what on earth I am to do there, armed only with a silver Böhm flute and some dozen of steel pens.

But Baltimore was henceforth his home, and for the remainder of his short life he was " engaged always in a threefold struggle, for health, for bread, and for a literary career." Often for months at a time he was forced to give up regular duties and to go away in search of recovery and renewed vitality. Flute and pen and lectures in schools enabled him to eke out a bare subsistence, though at the critical times of utter prostration the generous help of father and brother was necessary to prolong the struggle. The following sketch for a poem or possibly a passionate cry for help, which was found among his papers after his death, doubtless belongs to this period:

O Lord, if thou wert needy as I,
If thou should'st come to my door as I to
    thine,
If thou hungered so much as I
For that which belongs to the spirit,
For that which is fine and good,
Ah, friend, for that which is fine and
    good,
I would give it to thee if I had power.
For that which I want is, first, bread—
Thy decree, not my choice, that bread
    must be first;
Then music, then some time out of the
    struggle for bread to write my poems;
Then to put out of care Henry and Rob-
    ert, whom I love.
O my God, how little would put them out
    of care!

Sidney Lanier.

And his last letter to Paul H. Hayne, written in November, 1880, reveals the fact that these struggles continued to the last:

I have been wishing to write to you for a long time, and have *thought* several letters to you. But I could never tell you the extremity of illness, of poverty, and of unceasing toil, in which I have spent the last three years, and you would need only once to see the weariness with which I crawl to bed after a long day's work, and after a long night's work at the heels of it—and Sunday's just as well as other days—in order to find in your heart a full warrant for my silence. It seems incredible that I have printed such an unchristian quantity of matter—all too tolerably successful!—and secured so little money; and the wife and the four boys, who are so lovely that I would not think a palace good enough for them if I had it, make one's earnings seem all the less. . . . For six months past a ghastly fever has been taking possession of me, about 12 M., and holding my head under the surface of indescribable distress *for the next twenty hours*, subsiding only enough each morning to let me get on my working harness, but *never intermitting*. A number of tests shows it to be not the hectic so well known in consumption, and to this day it has baffled all the skill I could find in New York, Philadelphia, and here. I have myself been disposed to think it arose wholly from the bitterness of having to spend my time in making academic lectures and boys' books—potboilers all—when a thousand songs are singing in my heart, that will certainly kill me if I do not utter them soon. But I don't think this diagnosis has found favor with my practical physicians; and meanwhile I work on in such suffering as is piteous to see.

But his courage never failed him, and the amount of work he dispatched in the intervals between his hemorrhages is surprising. He began by making a thorough and systematic study of English literature, giving special attention to the Old-English period, and Langland, Chaucer, and Shakespeare, and then, "with a scholar's nice eagerness," he extended his reading widely in the natural sciences, philosophy, history, art, and music. "The trouble

192

with Poe was," he observed with keen discrimination, " he did not know enough. He needed to know a good many more things in order to be a great poet." Besides this, he attended rehearsals and played in the symphony concerts, edited books, prepared lectures, and wrote magazine articles and poems. This kind of work opened a new era in his artistic development; for though he could previously say, " So many great ideas for art are born to me each day, I am swept into the land of All-delight by their strenuous sweet whirlwind," he had rarely given expression to them. In music he needed neither art nor practice to fit him for its expression. He played as a mocking bird sings, with skill and repertoire furnished by nature. In poetry, however, he must first work out, adopt, and then endeavor to master a theory of formal verse, which was not popular; and as the conscientious artist in him refused permission to send forth any work but the best, he made his way slowly into the literary world. Fortunately combined with this tardiness of artistic poetic utterance were the consciousness of his powers and the patience to await the ripening time, "not taking thought of being late, so it give advantage to be more fit." In the meanwhile he is not without delightful experience and anticipation. "Day by day," he writes to his wife in February, 1870, "from my snow and my sunshine, a thousand vital elements rill through my soul. Day by day the secret deep forces gather, which will presently display themselves in bending leaf and waxy petal, and in useful fruit and grain."

In May, 1874, Lanier went again to Florida, commissioned by a railroad company to write an account of its scenery, climate, and history, and on his return he spent two months with his family at Sunny-

side, Ga. With a poet's eye and kin-
dled imagination he gazed upon the
ample fields and woods of his native
land, the old worn red hills, the zig-
zag - cornered fence with sassafras
and brambles dense, the dew-flashed
road of early morn, t h e woods
trembling through and through with
shimmering f o r m s, the mosses,
ferns, and flowers shy, the rustling
blades of corn whispering music to
his ear, caught their free, large spirit,
and sang with a new and fresh note
all his own the first song of his to
which the w o r l d gave heed—
" Corn." A personal visit to New
York in search of an editor who
would publish it for him only revealed the " wooden-headedness " of
some literary leaders, but this neither soured nor discouraged his
kindly and hopeful nature. " I remember," he writes, " that it has
always been so; that the new man
has always to work his way over
these Alps of Stupidity, much as

that ancient general crossed the actual Alps—splitting the rocks with
vinegar and fire—that is, by bitterness and suffering. D. V., I will
split them. . . . The more I am
thrown against these people here,
and the more reverses I suffer at
their hands, the more confident I am
of beating them finally. I do not
mean by 'beating' that I am in opposition to them, or that I hate
them or feel aggrieved with them;
no, they know no better, and they
act up to their light with wonderful
energy and consistency. I only
mean that I am sure of being able,
some day, to teach them better
things and nobler modes of thought
and conduct." After further effort,
however, " Corn " found a place in
Lippincott's Magazine for February, 1875, but the theme was too
commonplace and the treatment too
original to expect immediate general
recognition of its merits. To a select few it was evident that a new

singer had come. First of these was Mr. Gibson Peacock, editor of the *Philadelphia Evening Bulletin*, whose collegiate training and broad and generous culture, derived from wide reading in the best English literature, home and foreign travel, cultivation in music and dramatic criticism, enabled him to conduct a newspaper in which literary and artistic matters received serious treatment. Mr. Peacock's enthusiastic notice of the poem had a beneficent and far-reaching effect upon the young author's life—a strong and beautiful friendship between the two families, a series of letters from the poet, since published in the *Atlantic*, which relate " so humanly and beautifully the story of so precious a life," and acquaintance " with Charlotte Cushman, with Bayard Taylor, and with many another of the appreciators of art and literature who in those days frequented the little parlors in Walnut

Street." Lanier received now that broader association, friendship, and appreciation for which he had long been pining, and also "a little of the wine of success and of praise, without which no man ever does the very best he might," as he himself said, in speaking of what would have been of inestimable service to poor Henry Timrod's poetic faculty. These letters, edited with genuine appreciation and real skill by Mr. W. R. Thayer so as to let Lanier's personality, unconsciously drawn by himself, be as complete as possible, not only admit us into the fellowship of a poet, but they also disclose to us a man whose life was, in Milton's phrase, "a true poem." One delights to linger over them, to breathe their atmosphere, to catch their spirit.

The "Symphony" called forth another appreciative notice from Mr. Peacock, which was extensively copied in the Southern newspapers, and this time Bayard Taylor's generous voice swelled the chorus.

July 31, 1875, Lanier writes to Mr. Peacock: " Many thanks for Mr. Taylor's letter. I do hope I may be able to see him during the next month. Do you think a letter from me would reach him at Mattapoisett? For his estimate of my Symphony seems to me so full and generous that I think I will not resist the temptation to anticipate his letter to me. I will write also to Mr. Calvert to-morrow. His insight into a poet's internal working, as developed in his kind notice of me in the *Golden Age*, is at once wonderful and delightful." Mr. Taylor now became one of Lanier's most valued friends. He gave him freely counsel, sympathy, introductions to other writers, and it was at his suggestion that Lanier was selected to write the cantata for the opening of the Centennial Exposition in Philadelphia. w h i c h first brought his

199

name into general notice. From
Baltimore, January 8, 1876, he
writes to his wife:

Well then: God be praised that giveth
us the victory. I have late this afternoon
finished my third India paper, which was
a great labor and strain; and to-night we
have played a divine concert of Scandi-
navian music, whereof I inclose thee the
programme; and my heart is so full of
this heavenly melody that I cannot find
me any rest till I have in some wise enlarged me.

Moreover I have a charming piece of
news which—although thou art not yet
to communicate it to any one except Clifford—I cannot keep from thee. The
opening ceremonies of the Centennial
Exhibition will be very grand; and among
other things there are to be sung by a full
chorus (and played by the orchestra, under Thomas's direction) a hymn and a
cantata. Gen. Hawley, President of the
Centennial Commission, has written inviting me to write the latter (I mean the
poem; Dudley Buck, of New York, is to
write the music). Bayard Taylor is to
write the hymn. This is very pleasing to
me; for I am chosen as representative of
our dear South; and the matter puts my

200

name by the side of very delightful and
honorable ones, besides bringing me in
contact with many people I would desire
to know.

Mr. Buck has written me that he wants
the poem by January 15, which as I have
not yet had the least time for it, gives me
just seven days to write it in. I would
much rather have had seven months; but
God is great. Remember, thou and Cliff,
that this is not yet to be spoken of at all.

In a letter to Mr. Peacock, written
the 18th, he inclosed the first draft
of the cantata, saying: " Necessarily I had to think out the musical
conception as well as the poem, and
I have briefly indicated these along
the margin of each movement. I
have tried to make the whole as
simple and as candid as a melody of
Beethoven's; at the same time expressing the largest ideas possible,
and expressing them in such a way
as could not be offensive to any
modern soul. I particularly hope
you will like the Angel's song,
where I have endeavored to convey,

201

in one line each, the philosophies of Art, of Science, of Power, of Government, of Faith, and of Social Life. Of course I shall not expect that this will instantly appeal to tastes peppered and salted by Swinburne and that ilk; but one cannot forget Beethoven, and somehow all my inspirations come in these large and artless forms, in simple Saxon words, in unpretentious and purely intellectual conceptions; while nevertheless I felt, all through, the necessity of making a genuine song, and not a rhymed set of good adages, out of it. I adopted the trochees of the first movement because they *compel* a measured, sober, and meditative movement of the mind; and because, too, they are not the genius of our language. When the trochees cease and the land emerges as a distinct unity, then I fall into our native iambics." Of Mr. Buck he writes: "We have gotten on together with perfect harmony during the process of fitting together the words and the music, which has been wholly accomplished by letter."

The sky became somewhat brighter now; he was better paid for his work, receiving three hundred dollars for the "Psalm of the West," and his heart was gladdened by tokens of love and sympathy at home. From Macon he writes, April 27, 1876: "The Southern people make a great deal more of my appointment to write the cantata poem than I had ever expected, and it really seems to be regarded by them as one of the most substantial tokens of reconciliation yet evinced by that vague *tertium quid* which they are accustomed to represent to themselves under the general term of the 'North.' I am astonished, too, to find what a hold 'Corn' has taken upon all classes. Expressions come to me in great number from men whom I never supposed accessible

by any poetry whatever; and these
recognitions arrive hand in hand
with those from persons of the
highest culture. The *Tribune* notice of the cantata has been copied
by a great many Southern papers,
and I think it materially assisted in
starting the poem off properly;
though the people here are so enthusiastic in my favor at present that
they are quite prepared to accept
blindly anything that comes from
me. Of course I understand all this;
and any success seems cheap which
depends so thoroughly on local pride
as does my present position with the
South; yet in view of the long and
bitter struggle which I must make
up my mind to wage in carrying out
these extensions of poetic forms
about which all my thoughts now
begin to converge, it is pleasant to
find that I have at least the nucleus
of an audience which will be willing
to receive me upon the plane of mere
blind faith until time shall have giv-

en a more scientific basis to their understandings."

The publication of the cantata without the orchestral accompaniment, which the p o e t intended should be its chief distinction, occasioned an immense amount of ridicule, some good-natured, some spiteful. This criticism pained h i m deeply, though he quickly regained the serene heights on which he strove habitually to live. Not even to his friend Mr. Peacock did he show how sharp a sting it was, merely writing in a letter of April 27, in reference to one of the most vicious of these attacks: "Nothing rejoices me more than the inward perception how utterly the time and the frame of mind are passed by in which anything of this sort gives me the least disturbance. Six months ago this would have hurt me, even against my will. Now it seems only a little grotesque episode—just as when a few minutes ago I sat in

my father's garden here and heard
a catbird pause in the midst of the
most exquisite *roulades* and melodies, to mew, and then take up his
song again." But to his father he
wrote from New York, May 8,
more seriously : " My experience in
the varying judgments given about
poetry . . . has all converged upon
one solitary principle, and the experience of the artist in all ages is reported by history to be of precisely
the same direction. That principle
is that the artist shall put forth
humbly and lovingly, and without
bitterness against opposition, the
very best and highest that is within
him, utterly regardless of contemporary criticism. What possible
claim can contemporary criticism set
up to respect—that criticism which
crucified Jesus Christ, stoned Ste-
phen, hooted Paul for a madman,
tried Luther for a criminal, tortured
Galileo, bound Columbus in chains,
drove Dante into a hell of exile,

made Shakespeare write the sonnet 'When in disgrace with fortune and men's eyes,' gave Milton five pounds for 'Paradise Lost,' kept Samuel Johnson cooling his heels on Lord Chesterfield's doorstep, reviled Shelley as an unclean dog, killed Keats, cracked jokes on Glück, Schubert, Beethoven, Berlioz, and Wagner, and committed so many other impious follies and stupidities that a thousand letters like this could not suffice even to catalogue them?"

The reception given his poem continued to interest him deeply, and a few weeks later, May 27, he wrote to his wife, from Philadelphia, the following characteristic letter:

The papers are wondrously more respectful in their tone toward me, and it really seems as if my end of the seesaw was now rising steadily. I think the business has been of great value to all my artistic purpose, just at this stage of it; I have been compelled to throw aside every adventitious thing in the way of inspiration. God has been good to show

me at the outset in its most repulsive
form the fatal figure of contemporary
popularity, and to remind me how far
apart from it were Shakespeare, Beethoven, and Bach. Hereupon I feel already
resulting an immortal and unconquerable
toughness of fiber in the strings of my
harp, insomuch that if the world shall
attempt to play me—as it *does* play all the
popular men—it will only get its awkward
fingers sore. . . .

I inclose a slip or two for thy perusal.
The —— is marvelously another ——
than the contemptuous thing which a few
weeks ago dismissed my poem in three
lines. Of course all it says in this note is
simply that sort of nonsense which Stod-
dard affectionately calls "rot;" the ——
neither knows nor cares anything with
regard to music.

But this criticism had no tendency
to weaken the confidence which Lanier had acquired in his view of the
principles of art. In his period of
greatest uncertainty he had written
to his wife: "It is of little conse-
quence whether I fail; the *I* in the
matter is a small business. '*Que
mon nom soit flétri, que la France*

soit libre! ' quoth Danton ; which is
to say, interpreted by my environment : ' Let my name perish—the
poetry is good poetry and the music
is good music, and beauty dieth not,
and the heart that needs it will find
it.' " But a little remark in 1875
anent " Special Pleading " reveals
the fact that he is no longer agitated
over the matter. " In this little song
I have begun to dare to give myself
some freedom in my own peculiar
style, and have allowed myself to
treat words, similes, and meters with
such freedom as I desired. The result convinces me that I can do so
now safely." And as a natural result
he entered upon a period of greater
p r o d u c t i v i t y—"Clover," " The
Waving of the Corn," " The Bee,"
" The Song of the Chattahoochee,"
" The Revenge of Hamish," " The
Marshes of Glynn," and many more
following in rapid succussion those
already mentioned. Ten of these
poems were collected into a thin vol-

ume, covering o n l y ninety-four
pages, and published by the Lippin-
cotts in 1877, "but they strike the
whole r a n g e of his ambition."
Other writings during this period
were a series of papers on India for
Lippincott's Magazine, in which
to avoid arid encyclopedic treatment
and give naturalness to the adventures and descriptions, he called to
his aid a delightful imaginary Hindoo
friend—and his book on " Florida,"
published in 1876 by the Lippincott's, which cost him much travel,
fatigue, and labor. In a letter to
Paul H. Hayne he writes: "After
working day and night for the last
three months on the materials I had
previously collected, I have just finished the book. . . . This production is a sort of spiritualized guide-
book. . . . I have had to labor from
ten to fourteen hours a day, and the
confinement to the desk brought on
my old hemorrhages a month ago,
which quite threatened for a time to

suspend my work forever on this side the river." And yet this "pot-boiler," written under such conditions, is thoroughly characteristic of the author—cheerful, scientific, imaginative, full of delightful information, going out of the way to say a kind thing or quote a charming poem of a brother Southern poet, though it is melancholy reading when we call to mind a sentence in a letter written a little earlier to another friend: "My head and my heart are both so full of poems which the dreadful struggle for bread does not give me time to put on paper that I am often driven to headache and heartache purely for want of an hour or two to hold a pen."

His personal appearance at this time was striking, and fixed itself in the memory. "The name of Sidney Lanier," says Mr. E. C. Stedman, "brings him clearly to recollection as I saw him more than once in the study of our lamented

Sidney Lanier.

Deucalion—the host so buoyant and sympathetic—the Southerner, nervous and eager, with dark hair and s i l k e n beard, features delicately molded, p a l l i d complexion, and hands of the slender, white, artistic type." In a letter to the writer October 9, 1896, Mrs. Lanier says: " The profile portrait in the volume of 'Complete Poems'—taken from photograph of January, 1874—quite misrepresents his physique; for it suggests a man heavy built about the shoulders—the effect of a double-breasted coat of extraordinary thickness and other heaviest clothing—all worn to guard him from the rigor of the first Northern winter; while the attitude (inclining backward), in combination with this bulk of clothing, results in the wider discrepancy of an impression of portliness —the very opposite of his build and movement. A bow that is a-spring, a flying Mercury, more ethereal than John of Bologna's, with slender, yet uplifted chest—these rather convey the spirit of his earthly tenement. This profile, though it withholds the eye—brilliant and penetrating, yet tender—gives finely the expressive nostril, the brow, the ear, the fall of the silken-textured hair. More than any other it discloses to me the spiritual man, as the likeness taken at fifteen speaks the very spirit of the boy—that is, the original ambrotype and the direct photographic copies. No engraving of this face has approached success."

During the next two or three years Lanier was disappointed in various efforts to get permanent employment. In the summer and fall of 1876 he entertained the hope of filling " a sort of nondescript chair of Poetry and Music " in Johns Hopkins University, which was all the more tantalizing because of t h e President's evident inclination to make the offer. Next we hear of a

faint wish that Mr. Hayes would
appoint him to a consulship in the
south of France.   Then his kinsmen
and friends made a determined effort
to secure him a place in one of the
departments in Washington; but
September 27, 1877, he writes to
Mr. Peacock: " There does not appear the least hope of success here.
Three months ago the order was
given by Secretary Sherman that I
should have the first vacancy; but
the appointment clerk, who received
the order, is a singular person, and I
am told that there are rings within
rings in the department to such an
extent that vacancies are filled by
petty chiefs of division without ever
being reported at all to the proper
officers." November 3 he writes
again : " I have set on foot another
attempt to get a place in the Johns
Hopkins University; I also have a
prospect of employment as an assist-
ant at the Peabody Library here;
and there is still a possibility of a

committee clerkship in Washington. Meantime, however, I am just resuming work for the editors"—after nearly a year in search of health at Tampa, Fla., and in Georgia. He also now utilized his studies of English literature in a course of lectures on Elizabethan verse, which was delivered to a parlor class of thirty ladies. The enthusiastic reception accorded them induced him the following winter (1878–79) to give a Shakespeare c o u r s e, concerning which he wrote to Mr. Peacock November 5, 1878: " I wished to show, to such a class as I could assemble, how much more genuine profit there would be in *studying at first hand*, under the guidance of an enthusiastic interpreter, the writers and conditions of a particular epoch (for instance), than in reading any amount of commentary or in hearing any number of miscellaneous lectures on subjects which range from Palestine to pottery in the course of a week." Financially, both courses were a failure, but besides the great praise which they called forth there came at last, and almost too late, the long-desired appointment to a position in the university. It took the shape of a lectureship on English literature—the duties of which he was to assume the following scholastic year—and President Gilman's official notification reached the poet on his birthday, February 3, 1879, bringing with it the assurance, for the first time since his marriage twelve years before, of a fixed income. The summer of 1879 was spent at Rockbridge Alum Springs, in Virginia; and such was the rapidity with which he was now working that in six weeks he put into permanent form the results of his studies and investigations of the subject of versification. Used first as lectures, the work appeared in 1880 as "The Science of English Verse," and contained the theories which at times seemed to be dearer to the author than the success of his own poetry. Like other original treatises, it has called forth curiously opposite statements, ranging all the way from Mr. Stedman's, " That remarkable piece of analysis, ' The Science of English Verse,' serves little purpose except, like Coleridge's metaphysics, to give us further respect for its author's intellectual powers," to Prof. Sill's " The work of Sidney Lanier on English verse may be recommended as the only one that has ever made any approach to a rational view of the subject. Nor are the standard ones overlooked in making this assertion." A modification of the latter view seems more likely to prevail, as not a few are inclined to accept it as the best working theory for English verse from Cædmon to Tennyson that has yet been produced. This is specially true of those who stand

"on that middle ground where Lanier dwelt, halfway between verse
and music." Fortunately, however,
Lanier was able to throw off the
shackles of his *Science*, as Poe was
of his *Rationale*, though not so uni-
formly nor so completely as Poe. It
would have been better, however, if
Lanier had ever kept in mind some
of the closing words of this treatise,
"that the matters herein treated are
only in the nature of hints, . . . and
by no means laws. For the artist
in verse there is no law : the perception and love of beauty constitute
the whole outfit ; and what is herein
set forth is to be taken merely as
enlarging that perception and exalt-
ing that love. In all cases the appeal is to the ear ; but the ear should,
for that purpose, be educated up to
the highest possible plane of culture."

With great rapidity and evenness
of work Lanier edited also between
1878 and 1881 a series of books for

boys, which appeared as follows:
" Froissart," 1879 ; " King Arthur,"
1880 ; " Mabinogion," 1881 ; and
" Percy," 1882. The editing shows
not only knowledge, taste, and conscientious labor; but also reveals
that genuine love for the old, the
chivalrous, and the romantic which
springs from a natural affinity. He
dearly loved old English worthies,
chroniclers, and poets, while knights
and knightly deeds captivated his
imagination and influenced his conduct. The " Introductions," written in admirably pure English, are
fine specimens of a didactic narrative
style, and, like everything the author
wrote, almost every sentence discloses some feature of his mind or
character. It will doubtless interest
many to read again his last words
to American b o y s, written at
" Camp Robin," near Asheville, N.
C., a few weeks before his departure: " He who walks in the way
these following ballads point will

be manful in necessary fight, fair in
trade, loyal in love, generous to the
poor, tender in the household, pru-
dent in living, plain in speech, merry upon occasion, simple in behav-
ior, and honest in all things. In
this trust and this knowledge I now
commend my young countrymen to
' The Boy's Percy.' "

Many other things, too, engaged
his attention at this time. December 21, 1878, he writes, "I am in
the midst of two essays on Anglo-
Saxon poetry ; " and then in a letter
to a friend a few months before he
died we see how he was employing
his many-sided genius and manifold
activities :

My lectures take all my time, and I
cannot write you. I had not thought
they would be so laborious, but I find the
numerous illustrations of antique thought
and habit require a great deal of research, and each lecture is a good week's
work for a well man. And when I contemplate the other things I am waiting to
do, many of them half done, to-wit: (1)

my "Hymns of the Marshes," nearly
complete, whereof you have the "Marshes of Glynn" and the little song of
"Trees and the Master;" (2) my "Clover
and Other Poems," now quite ready for
the press; (3) my "Credo and Other
Poems," a thick volume, all in memoranda, ready to be written out in a few
weeks; (4) my "Choral Symphony," for
chorus and orchestra, being my "Psalm
of the West," with music; (5) my "Symphony Life," in four movements—first,
childhood; second, youth; third, manhood; fourth, old age; (6) my "Symphony of the Plantation," being the old and
the new life of the negro, in music; (8)
my "Girl's Paston Letters," now in my
desk, half prepared; (9) my "Boy's Mon-
strelet," also in desk ready to arrange;
(10) my "Boy's Gesta Romanorum"—
when I contemplate these, now lying
upon my hands in actual forms of one
sort or another, without daring to think
of books merely projected, I fall to won-
dering whether I have any business or
right to wait, whether I had not better
go and borrow five thousand, ten thousand dollars—which could be so easily
repaid in five years (the copyrights of
the "Boy's Froissart" and "King Arthur" would have done it if I had not

been obliged to sell them), and put myself in heaven at once, with nothing but
poetry to write and two years of freedom
from slavery to butcher and baker.

But at the time he was preparing
these lectures and penning this letter he was being quickly consumed
by the final fever, which, Dr. Ward
informs us, set in in May, 1880.
The following winter brought a hand
to hand battle for life, and in December it was thought that he was at
death's door. Nevertheless before
April 1, 1881, he had delivered the
twelve lectures—there were to have
been twenty—which were later published under the title of " The English Novel." "A few of the earlier
lectures," continues Dr. Ward, " he
penned himself; the rest he was
obliged to dictate to his wife. With
the utmost care of himself, going in
a closed carriage and sitting during
his lecture, his strength was so exhausted that the struggle for breath
in the carriage on his return seemed

each time to threaten the end. Those who heard him listened with a sort of fascinated terror, as in doubt whether the hoarded breath would suffice to the end of the hour. It was in December of this winter, when too feeble to raise the food to his mouth, with a fever temperature of 104 degrees, that he penciled his last and greatest poem, 'Sunrise,' one of his projected series of the 'Hymns of the Marshes.' It seemed as if he were in fear that he would die with it unuttered."

Perhaps a little note on "Hamlet" which he left in his desk will throw some light on the cheerfulness and serenity with which he continued his work to the very last:

The grave scene is the most immense conception of all tragedy to me; it is the apparition of death upon a world which has not yet learned the meaning of life: how bleak it is, it is only skulls and regret; there is no comfort in it. But death, my God! it is the sweetest and dearest of all the angels to him who understands.

After giving this course of lectures he rallied enough to go to New York to complete arrangements with his publisher for bringing out the remaining volumes of the Boy's series. But while there his illness became so aggravated that "his medical adviser pronounced tent life in a pure, high climate to be the last hope." His brother Clifford took him to Richmond Hill, three miles from Asheville, N. C., where his father and wife joined them, his own devoted wife having already taken her place as nurse by his bedside. No one can record the end in simpler or better-chosen words than Dr. Ward has done: "As the passing weeks brought no improvement to the sufferer, he started August 4 on a carriage journey across the mountains with his wife to test the climate of Lynn, Polk County, N. C. There deadly illness attacked him. No return was possible, and Clifford was summoned by telegraph, and assisted his father in removing the encampment to Lynn. Deceived by hope, and pressed by business cares, Clifford went home August 24, and the father and his wife five days later, expecting to return soon. Mrs. Lanier's own words, as written in the brief 'annals' of his life furnished me, will tell the end: 'We are left alone (August 29) with one another. On the last night of the summer comes a change. His love and immortal will hold off the destroyer of our summer yet one more week, until the forenoon of September 7, and then falls the frost, and that unfaltering will renders its supreme submission to the adored will of God.'" This was a life ideal in its simplicity, serenity, and purity, and inspiring in its heroic endeavor, lofty aspiration, and Christian faith. No mantle of charity had to be thrown over anything that Sidney Lanier ever said or did. And it is pleasing to know that as he lay awake in the weary watches of the night beautiful thoughts and poetic fancies were his blessed companions. By the kind permission of Mrs. Lanier I am permitted to give just here one of these—a little poem that has never been published before—" written in ' Camp Robin,' on the mountain side near Asheville, summer of 1881 : "

I was the earliest bird awake,
It was awhile before dawn, I believe,
But somehow I saw round the world,
And the eastern mountain top did not
  hinder me.
And I knew of the dawn by my heart, not
  by mine eyes.

After his heart was forever gladdened by a more glorious dawn the body was taken back to Baltimore and laid away in the Greenmount cemetery. In October the Faculty and students of Johns Hopkins University held a memorial service, but it would seem that only a few at that time were more than dimly

226

conscious of their great loss. At
any rate within a very few years, on
February 3, 1888, a much larger and
more appreciative gathering, drawn
from many places, assembled in the
same university to witness the un-
veiling and presentation of his bust,
and to pay distinguished honor to his
memory in addresses, in papers of
critical appreciation, in readings from
his poems, in poetical tributes and letters from leading American writers
—all of which President Gilman
published as a " Memorial of Sidney
Lanier." For in this short time his
two chief productions had appeared
—" The English Novel," in 1883,
and the " Poems," edited by his wife,
in 1884. The latter was also accompanied by a " Memorial," written by
Dr. William Hayes Ward, which
has been of no little service in calling attention to the poet's manly
struggle, beautiful life, and high
achievement. And now that his life
and his life work had been present-

ed with at least partial completeness
not a few finer minds and nobler
natures were instinctively attracted
to both, and many other articles, re-
views and studies, have followed in
quick succession. Of those in England one in the *Spectator* is deserv-
ing of special mention. A *replica*
of the bust presented to the Johns
Hopkins University, both gifts of
his kinsman, Mr. Charles Lanier,
was unveiled at the poet's birthplace
October 17, 1890, and since 1895
" Select Poems of Sidney Lanier,"
a neat little volume carefully edited
with introduction, notes, and bibli-
ography, by Prof. Morgan Callaway, Jr., PhD., of the University of
Texas, has greatly facilitated acquaintance with some of his finer
poems. The Chautauquans, too, of
the class of 1898 have called themselves " The Laniers," in honor of
the poet and his brother, and there
are many other indications of an increasing interest in his life and in his

writings. This interest will doubtless be still more widely extended
when the complete story is given
to the world; for we have here the
promise of a rich and interesting bi-
ography, and it is gratifying to learn
that there is ample material for it—
in the way of letters to and from
friends, those to his wife being considered by some who have seen or
heard them "superior to Shelley's,"
pencil jottings in notebooks, on bill-
heads, on envelopes, on any bit of
paper at hand, copious memoranda
for poems, notes for lectures, besides
the abundant revelations of himself
in his writings. And no one is so
worthily fitted or properly prepared
for this undertaking as the poet's
wife, for, as Miss Mary E. Burt has
aptly said,

Mrs. Lanier carries the poetic atmosphere, the ideal way of looking at things,
the uplift of great association and rare
good breeding not "teased by small mixt
social claims," wherever she goes. No

poet's wife ever nursed his Muse so jealously, or after his death went on living his life out for him so faithfully. The genius of Sidney Lanier finds a secure, a charming, an intelligent continuance in his wife's interpretation of him.

The foundation of Lanier's superb equipment, it would seem, was music. This was his supreme nature-gift, his earliest passion, his abiding love. Music echoes through his books; music dominates his theories of poetry. "The 'imagery' of music—'notes' and 'tones' and 'melodies' and 'harmonies' and 'tone-colors'—is his natural language." Nor does he in the least misread himself when in 1873 he writes to a friend: "Whatever turn I may have for art is purely *musical*, poetry being with me *a mere tangent into which I shoot sometimes*." He lived in a concord of sweet sounds. A little fragment headed "The beauty of holiness: the holiness of beauty," left among his papers,

gives a unique revelation of how
essentially musical was his nature:
"A holy tune was in my soul when
I fell asleep; it was going when I
awoke. This melody is always
moving along the background of
my spirit. If I wish to compose,
I abstract my attention from the
thoughts which occupy the front of
the stage, the *dramatis personæ* of
the moment, and fix myself upon
the deeper scene in the rear." The
following letter, written to his wife
from New York August 15, 1870,
will perhaps give a faint conception
of the joy of his soul while listening
to the finest music:

Flutes and horns and violins, celestial
sighs and breaths slow-drawn, penetrated
with that heavenly woe which the deep
heart knoweth when it findeth not room
in the world for its too great love, and is
worn with fasting for the beloved; fine
purity fiercely attacked by palpitating
fascinations, and bracing herself and
struggling and fighting therewith, till
what is maidenly in a man is become all

grimy and sweat-beaded like a warrior.
Dear Love, shot by some small arrow
and in pain with the wound thereof; divine lamentations, far-off blowings of
great winds, flutterings of tree and flower
leaves, and air troubled with wing beats
of birds or spirits; floatings hither and
thither of strange incenses and odors and
essences; warm floods of sunlight, cool
gleams of moonlight, faint enchantments
of twilight, delirious dances, noble
marches, processional chants, hymns of
joy and of grief—ah [all these came to
me] last night, in the first chair next to
Thomas's Orchestra.

All this is clearly recognized in
the beautiful tribute to his musical
genius given by Asger Hamerik,
his director for six years in the Peabody Symphony Orchestra in Baltimore:

To him as a child in his cradle music
was given, the heavenly gift to feel and
to express himself in tones. His human
nature was like an enchanted instrument,
a magic flute or the lyre of Apollo,
needing but a breath or a touch to send
its beauty out into the world. It was indeed irresistible that he should turn with

those poetical feelings which transcend language to the penetrating gentleness of the flute, or the infinite passion of the violin; for there was an agreement, a spiritual correspondence between his nature and theirs, so that they mutually absorbed and expressed each other. In his hands the flute no longer remained a mere material instrument, but was transformed into a voice that set heavenly harmonies into vibration. Its tones developed colors, warmth, and a low sweetness of unspeakable poetry, they were not only true and pure, but poetic, allegoric as it were, suggestive of the depths and heights of being and of the delights which the earthly ear never hears and the earthly eye never sees. No doubt his firm faith in these lofty idealities gave him the power to present them to our imaginations, and thus by the aid of the higher language of music to inspire others with that sense of beauty in which he constantly dwelt. His conception of music was not reached by an analytic study of note by note, but was intuitive and spontaneous; like a woman's reason he felt it so because he felt it so, and his delicate perception required no more logical form of reasoning. His playing appealed alike to the musically learned

and to the unlearned, for he would mag-
netize the listener; but the artist felt in
his performance the superiority of the
momentary living inspiration to all the
rules and shifts of mere technical schol-
arship. His art was not only the art of
art, but an art above art. I will never
forget the impression he made on me
when he played the flute concerta of Emil
Hartmann at a Peabody Symphony concert in 1878—his tall, handsome, manly
presence, his flute breathing noble sorrows, noble joys, the orchestra softly re-
sponding. The audience was spellbound.
Such distinction, such refinement! He
stood, the master, the genius!

In rare conjunction with this exquisite musical nature was the philosophic and scientific mind. Lanier,
too, followed Solomon's direction,
" Get learning, get understanding,"
recognizing that the road lay
" through application, study, and
thought." And he also belonged,
as we have seen, to the modern
world of scholarly research and scientific inquiry. He was, moreover,
an inventor, a lover of the natural

sciences, and his instincts and ambitions were of this nineteenth century. " Science," he observes, " instead of being the enemy of poetry, is its quartermaster and commissary." And to young poets he says : " You need not dream of winning the attention of sober people with your poetry unless that poetry and your soul behind it are informed and saturated with at least the largest final conceptions of current science." To comfort his wife in the period of his greatest uncertainty he had written : " Know, then, disappointments were inevitable, and will still come until I have fought the battle which every great artist has had to fight since time began. This—dimly felt while I was doubtful of my vocation and powers—is clear as the sun to me now that I *know*, through the fiercest tests of life, that I am in soul, and shall be in life and utterance, a great poet." " But," says Dante, " the best conceptions cannot be, save where science and genius are;" and Lanier, believing this implicitly, held in reserve his powers of expression till he could formulate a scientific theory of the art of versification. He was confident of his own genius, but at the same time "possessed by the deepest conviction that the beauty of the art of poetry, like all other beauty, had its foundation in law." He therefore proceeded to construct a comprehensive philosophy of formal and substantial beauty in literature—two parts of which appear in "The Science of English Verse" and "The English Novel," the former dealing with the forms of poetic execution, the latter with the development of personality.

"The Science of English Verse" owes its origin to the conviction, expressed in a letter to Mr. Stedman, that "in all directions the poetic art was suffering from the shameful circumstance that criticism was without a scientific basis for even the most elementary of its judgments." Lanier's reasoning then seems to have been, as I gather more particularly from " The English Novel," thus—all accounts, scientific, religious, and historical, agree that the progress of things is *from* chaos or formlessness *to* form, then from one form to many, verse and prose for instance developing from the one-formed to the many-formed, that as all art is a congeries of forms each art must have its peculiar science, and always we have in a true sense the art of an art and the science of that art, hence the science of verse is no collection of rules for making verse, no more than Prof. Huxley's work on the crayfish is a cookery book. If one is disposed to say "*As for me, I would rather continue to write verse from pure instinct*," as a valued friend who had won a considerable place in contemporary authorship expressed himself to Lanier, his answer was : " This fallacy —of supposing we do a thing by instinct simply because we *learned* to do it unsystematically and without formal teaching—seems a curious enough climax to the misconceptions of literary science."

In the preface to this work we get Lanier's other point of view : " If Puttenham in the sixteenth century could wish to make the art of poetry ' vulgar for all Englishmen's use,' such a desire in the nineteenth must needs become a religious aspiration. For under our new dispensation the preacher must soon be a poet, as were the preachers before him under the old. To reach an audience of a variety so prodigious as to range from the agnostic to the devotee no forms of less subtlety than those of tone can be effective. A certain wholly unconscious step already made in this direction by society gives a confirmation of fact to this view which perhaps no argument

238

can strengthen: I mean the now
common use of music as a religious
art. Music already occupies one end
of the Church; the same inward
need will call poetry to the other."
For in this poet's estimation poetry
is not to be classified with placid indifference as polite literature, nor
does the poet write to amuse.
"That all worthy poets," he continues, "belong substantially to the
school of David, that it is the poet's
business to keep the line of men
touching shoulders with each other,
that the poet is in charge of all
learning to convert it into wisdom,
and that therefore a treatise on the
poet's method is in its last result a
sort of disciplinary preparation and
magister choralis for the congrega-
tion as well as for the preacher of
the future—these will not be regarded as merely visionary propositions,
and perhaps will be here accepted
at least as giving a final unity to the
principles now to be set forth."

Sidney Lanier.

The following short abstract taken from Prof. Charles W. Kent's excellent "Study of Lanier's Poems" will give a fair conception of his method:

Lanier in the "Science of English Versification," after discussing the four possible sound-relations, duration, intensity, pitch, and tone-color, shows that only three exact coördinations are possible— namely, duration, pitch, and tone-color, or their effects, rhythm, time, and color. He then points out that music and verse differ only in the means by which the coordination of rhythm, time, and tone-color are made—namely, in the case of music by *musical sounds*, and in the case of verse by *spoken words*. Rhythm is then discussed, the principle of accent as the basis of rhythm is discarded, and time is postulated and defended as the essential basis. This established, the quantity of a syllable, the grouping of sounds into bars as units of measure, and the broader grouping by phrases, by lines or meters, by stanzas and by poems, are treated fully. The phrase grouping may be effected in various ways—for instance, by logical pause, by alliteration, by logical accent, etc.

240

Sidney Lanier.

The essential difference of Lanier's theory from that generally received is this: that rhythm in verse is precisely the same as rhythm in music, and that rhythm in music consists of exact time relations among sounds and silences. Hence the office of accent cannot begin until rhythm is established, and then its office is limited simply to grouping into bars. But both bars and accent are unessential to verse. Rhythmic pronunciation and logical accents must not be confounded. Using the musical notation, the author shows that bars contain a given number of notes of a fixed length. In making out the proper number of units of time, absence of time must be supplied by pauses of definite length. The bar may contain any number of units of time in theory, but practically, rhythm containing three units or three rhythm, and rhythm containing four units or four rhythm, are the ones occurring, and of these the three rhythm is by far the most popular in English.

Greater freedom, it is intended, should hereby be given to poetry, so that there may be no other limitations than the capacity of the human ear to comprehend or coördinate the grouping of the sounds. "There is certainly nothing more interesting in Lanier's book," says Thomas Wentworth Higginson, " than when he shows that just as a Southern negro will improvise on the banjo daring variations, such as would, if Haydn employed them, be called high art; so Shakespeare often employed the simplest devices of sound, such as are familiar in nursery songs, and produced effects which are lyrically indistinguishable from those of Mother Goose." After calling attention, then, to the prevalence and universal tacit recognition of tune in ordinary speech, Lanier adds :

Once we get a fair command of all these subtle resources of speech-tunes, once we have trained our ears to recognize and appreciate them properly, once we have learned to use them in combination with the larger rhythm, which are easily within the compass of our English tongue, what strides may we not take toward that goal, of the complete expression of all the complex needs or hopes or despairs of modern life, which ever glitters through the clouds of commonplace before the eyes of the fervent artist!

But with Lanier there was no intention of allowing this liberty to go back into formlessness again. One of his latest utterances on this subject emphasizes his position. " Once for all remembering the dignity of form as we have traced it, remembering the relations of science as the knowledge of forms, of art as the creator of beautiful forms, of religion as the aspiration toward unknown forms and the unknown form-giver, let us abandon this unworthy attitude toward form, toward science, toward technic, in literary art, which has so long sapped our literary endeavor." Lanier died too young to give perfect expression to his scientific theories in beautiful poetic creations, though it must be granted that he was making marvelous progress toward the last. This is all the more necessary to keep in

243

mind since Mr. Stedman has said
that " Lanier's difficulties were ex-
plained by the very traits which
made his genius unique. His musical faculty was compulsive. It inclined him to override Lessing's law
of the distinctions of art and to essay
in language feats that only the gamut can render possible."

In a recent letter, October 9, 1896,
Mrs. Lanier says: "As Mr. Lanier's
very first book has long been out of
print, so for three years has been
his latest one, ' The English Novel,'
but under more hopeful conditions
of recovery. Under that title were
published the twelve lectures delivered in 1881 at Johns Hopkins University, a course named by the lec-
turer, ' From Æschylus to George
Eliot, the Development of Personality.' The book-title has not con-
veyed the purpose of the lectures,
for the novel was chosen only as the
literary form in which the development of personality could best be

Sidney Lanier.

studied in contrast to its crude and
faint expression in the Æschylean
drama. In a forthcoming revised
edition the new sub-title will clearly
indicate this purpose, while a great
number of errors will be corrected.
The publication of these lectures
was urged in 1882 by friends who
had listened to them. At the time,
and for long afterwards, I was quite
disabled and could exercise no dis-
cretion, and I followed the counsel
of one who, after a too cursory examination, believed that they would
need 'only careful proof reading.'
My inexperience kept me from seeing that some editing was indispen-
sable with an unrevised first draught
of a work that had been shaped and
penned in the feebleness of mortal
illness; so it was committed to the
generous care of a friend, without
giving him liberty to lay any doubtful question before me during a long
seclusion under rest 'treatment.' A
multitude of mistakes ensued; some

from the copyist's unfamiliarity with
the handwriting and misunderstand-
ing of the imperfect manuscript;
others from the editor's uncertainties
as to Mr. Lanier's final wish at various points. When these came to
my notice the book was in circulation, with plates stereotyped, and the
only complete remedy lay in new
plates. After thirteen years this
remedy is about to be applied, and
the coming December, it is hoped,
will see ' The English Novel' again
in circulation. It will have new and
better type, a full index, and paragraphs that were omitted in the earlier edition." " The Science of
English Verse " may prove to be of
more permanent value; but at present " The English Novel " is a far
more interesting work not only to
the general reader, but also to the
student of literature. It has the
rare value of being stimulating,
suggestive, and helpful at the same
time, though its higher worth is in

the author's historical treatment of
the development of personality, in
his eloquent presentation of his theories of art and in much incidental
interpretative and illuminating criticism. Prof. Morgan Callaway's
synopsis, though brief, adequately
presents the author's purpose. He
says: "According to the author's
statement the purpose of the book is,
first, to inquire what is the special
relation of the novel to the modern
man, by virtue of which it has become a paramount literary form;
and secondly, to illustrate this abstract inquiry, when completed, by
some concrete readings in the greatest of modern English novelists."
Addressing himself to the former,
Lanier attempts to prove (1) that
our time, when compared with that
of Æschylus, shows an "enormous
growth in the personality of man;"
(2) that what we moderns call physical science, music, and the novel all
had their origin at practically the

same time, about the middle of the seventeenth century ; and (3) " that the increase of personalities thus going on has brought about such complexities of relation that the older forms of expression were inadequate to them ; and that the resulting necessity has developed the wonderfully free and elastic form of the modern novel out of the more rigid Greek drama, through the transition form of the Elizabethan drama." Then by way of illustration follows a detailed study of several of the novels of George Eliot, whom Lanier considered the greatest of English novelists.

Of vital interest, too, is Lanier's attitude to the effect of science upon the art of poetry and " art for art's sake." During his lifetime poetry was threatened with defeat by betrayal within her own household and with destruction from the strongly intrenched camp of modern science. It was more than in-

timated in certain quarters that the
poet, the novelist, and all imaginative literature, along with faith and
a few other superfluous winged and
mist-clad idealities, were to be abol-
ished. How a mind "as truly philosophically and scientifically accurate as it was poetically sensuous
and imaginative" would regard such
an intimation is to be seen in this
volume. After pointing out that
while gravitation, oxygen, electro-
magnetism, the atomic theory, the
spectroscope, the siren, are being
evolved, the "Ode to St. Cecilia,"
the "Essay on Man," "Manfred,"
"A Man's a Man, for A' That,"
the "Ode on Immortality," "In
Memoriam," the "Ode to a Nightingale," "The Psalm of Life" are
being written, and after calling attention to Goethe, "at once pursuing science and poetry," he adds:
"Now, if we examine the course
and progress of this poetry, born
thus within the very grasp and maw

of this terrible science, it seems to
me that we find—as to the *substance*
of poetry—a steadily increasing confidence and joy in the mission of
the poet, in the sacredness of faith
and love and duty and friendship
and marriage, and the sovereign
fact of man's personality, while as
to the *form* of the poetry we find
that just as science has pruned our
faith (to make it more faithful), so
it has pruned our poetic form and
technic, cutting away much unpro-
ductive wood and efflorescence and
creating finer reserves and richer
yields." There was no fear in his
mind that science would ever find
out the Almighty unto perfection or
uncloak the mysteries of the uni-
verse. Yet, as with all serious, re-
flecting souls, when some of the
latter obtruded their ghastly presence into the forefront of his observation, the former at times seemed
to be far away, as the following unpublished fragment discloses : " In

the lily, the sunset, the mountain, and the rosy hues of all life it is easy to trace God. But it is in the dust that goes up from the unending battle of things that we lose him. Forever through the ferocities of storms, the malice of the never-glutted oceans, the savagery of human wars, the inexorable barbarities of accident, of earthquake, and mysterious disease one hears the voice of man crying: '*Where art thou, my dear Lord and Master?*'"

In the quiet hours of meditation and of love the answer came to Lanier, as it comes to all those

> Godly hearts, that, grails of gold,
> Still the blood of faith do hold.

"I have a boy whose eyes are as blue as your Aëthra's," he writes to Paul H. Hayne. "Every day when my work is done I take him in my strong arms and lift him up and pore in his face. The intense repose, penetrated somehow with a thrilling mystery of *potential activ-*

ity which dwells in his large, open eye, teaches me new things. I say to myself: 'Where are the strong arms in which I, too, might lay me and repose, and yet be full of the fire of life?' And always through the twilight come answers from the other world: 'Master! Master! there is one—Christ; in his arms we rest!'"

But his highest joy and deepest satisfaction in contemplating the "Crystal Christ" were attained through art. He was neither the agnostic nor the religionist. "The Church is too hot," he says in an unpublished fragment—"The Beauty of Holiness: the Holiness of Beauty"—"and Nothing is too cold. I find my proper temperature in art. Art offers to me a method of adoring the sweet Master, Jesus Christ, without the straitness of a creed which confines my genuflections and without the vacuity of doubt which numbs them. An unspeak-

252

able gain has come to me in simply
turning a certain phrase the other
way. The beauty of holiness becomes a new and wonderful saying
to me when I figure it to myself in
reverse as the holiness of beauty.
This is like opening a window of
dark-stained glass and letting in a
flood of white light. I thus keep
upon the walls of my soul a church
wall rubric which has been somewhat clouded by the expiring
breaths of creeds dying their natural
deaths. For in art there is no doubt.
My heart beat all last night without
my supervision, for I was asleep.
My heart did not doubt a throb. I
left it beating when I slept; I found
it beating when I awoke. It is thus
with art: it beats in my sleep. A
holy tune was in my soul when I
fell asleep; it was going when I
awoke. This melody is always
moving along in the background of
my spirit."

In his soul, however, artistic beau-

ty and moral beauty are twin stars
that give a single light. "Let any
sculptor," he says in this book, "hew
out the most ravishing combination
of tender curves and spheric softness that ever stood for woman;
yet if the lip have a certain fullness
that hints of the flesh, if the brow
be insincere, if in the minutest particular the physical beauty suggests
a moral ugliness, that sculptor—unless he be portraying a moral ugliness for a moral purpose—may as
well give over his marble for paving
stones. Time, whose judgments
are inexorably moral, will not accept
his work. For, indeed, we may say
that he who has not yet perceived
how artistic beauty and moral beauty are convergent lines which run
back into a common ideal origin,
and who is therefore not afire with
moral beauty just as with artistic
beauty; that he, in short, who has
not come to that stage of quiet and
eternal frenzy in which the beauty

of holiness and the holiness of beauty mean one thing, burn as one fire, shine as one light within him, he is not yet the great artist."

Nay, he does not hesitate to inculcate a moral purpose nor lose sight of the higher fact that a man's words and deeds should be in harmony—a "perfect life in perfect labor writ," was his own ideal. "Cannot one say with authority to the young artist, whether working in stone, in color, in tones, or in character forms of the novel: so far from dreading that your moral purpose will interfere with your beautiful creation, go forward in the clear conviction that, unless you are suffused—soul and body, one might say—with that moral purpose which finds its largest expression in love—that is, the love of all things in their proper relation—unless you are suffused with this love, do not dare to meddle with beauty; unless you are suffused

with beauty, do not dare to meddle
with truth; unless you are suffused
with truth, do not dare to meddle
with goodness. In a word, unless
you are suffused with truth, wisdom, goodness, and love, abandon
the hope that the ages will accept
you as an artist."

This little "note" for a Johns
Hopkins lecture may be taken as
his final word on this subject: "A
man of mere cleverness can reach a
certain point of progressive technic,
but after that it is only moral nature
which can carry him farther forward, which can teach him anything."

As a critic Lanier was more remarkable for penetration and apt
characterization of particular authors
than for range of sympathy and unerring judgment. He was often
illuminative and interpretative, as
when he says of William Morris:
" He caught a crystal cupful of yellow light of sunset, and, persuading

himself to deem it wine, drank it
with a sort of smile." And when
he comes to speak of Shelley he is
even more felicitous: "In truth,
Shelley appears always to have labored under an essential immaturi-
ty; it is very possible that if he
had lived a hundred years he would
never have become a man; he was
penetrated with modern ideas, but
penetrated as a boy would be—crude-
ly, overmuch, and with a constant
tendency to the extravagant and illogical, so that I call him the modern
boy." He indicated with aptest
words the weak places in Milton and
Tennyson and Emerson. But his
observation on Swinburne, "He in-
vited me to eat; the service was
silver and gold, but no food therein
save pepper and salt," is not so happy; for, as the Spectator has pointed
out, no one can say of "Atalanta in
Calydon," or even of "Bothwell,"
that there is nothing in it but condi-
ment. And, on the other hand, the

service is by no means always of
silver and gold, for the Swinburne
verbiage is often so oppressive that
the alloy presses itself on the attention a great deal more than the
precious metal. The criticism on
Thackeray is still wider of the
mark. To speak of "the sub-acid
satiric mood of Thackeray"—to
stress it as a "mood of hate" and
to say that "Thackeray and his
school, when they speak of drawing
a man as he is—of the natural, etc.,
in art—would mean drawing a man
as he appears in such a history as the
daily newspaper gives"—is to misread the tenderest heart and to mis-
judge the finest art of all the great
English novelists. The reason why
Lanier could not see that

> If he smiled,
> His smile had more of sadness than of
> mirth,
> But more of love than either,

was rather a matter of temperament
than of heart. Nor was there be-

tween them that mental affinity which drew Lanier so strongly to George Eliot. Not only her philosophic and scientific mind appealed to him, but also her attitude toward life — weltanschauung — was congenial to his manner of thinking. This, it would seem, accounts for the position he has assigned her, as attaining the height thus far reached in fiction of subtle portrayal of human personality—in the following paragraph: " You will observe that of the two commandments in which the Master summed up all duty and happiness—namely, to love the Lord with all our heart and to love our neighbor as ourself—George Eliot's whole life and work were devoted to the exposition of the latter. She has been blamed for devoting so little attention to the former. As for me, I am too heartily grateful for the stimulus of human love which radiates from all her works to feel any sense of lack or regret. This, after

Sidney Lanier.

all—the general stimulus along the
line of one's whole nature—is the
only true benefit of contact with the
great; more than this is hurtful.
Nowadays you do not want an author to tell you how many times a
day to pray, to prescribe how many
inches wide shall be the hem of
your garment. This the Master
never did; too well he knew the
growth of personality which *would*
settle these matters, each for itself;
too well he knew the subtle hurt of
all such violations of modern indi-
vidualism; and after our many
glimpses of the heartiness with
which George Eliot recognized the
fact and function of human personality one may easily expect that she
never attempted to teach the world
with a rule and square, but desired
only to embody in living form those
prodigious generalizations in which
the Master's philosophy, considered
purely as philosophy, surely excelled all other systems. In fine, if

Sidney Lanier.

I try to sum up the whole work of
this great and beautiful spirit, which
has just left us, in the light of all the
various views I have presented in
these lectures, where we have been
tracing the growth of human personality from Æschylus, through Plato,
Socrates, the contemporary Greek
mind, through t h e Renaissance,
Shakespeare, Richardson, Fielding,
down to Dickens and our author. I
find all the numerous threads of
thought which have been put before
you gathered into one if I say that
George Eliot shows man what he
may be in terms of what he is."

But the best and most trenchant
of Lanier's criticisms is that on Walt
Whitman, though his condemnation
of the author of " Leaves of Grass "
was not so sweeping as it appears
in the first edition of " The English
Novel." The following paragraph
from his original manuscript, occurring between " democratic and form-
less " and " I need quote but a few

scraps" (page 44, l. 6.) was omitted, but will find its proper place in the forthcoming edition :

But let me first carefully disclaim and condemn all that flippant and sneering tone which dominates so many discussions of Whitman. While I differ from him utterly as to every principle of artistic procedure; while he seems to me the most stupendously mistaken man in all history as to what constitutes true democracy and the true advance of art and man while I am immeasurably shocked at the sweeping invasions of those reserves which depend on the very personality I have so much insisted upon, and which the whole consensus of the ages has considered more and more sacred with every year of growth in delicacy; yet, after all these prodigious allowances, I owe some keen delight to a certain combination of bigness and *naïveté* which make some of Whitman's passages so strong and taking; and indeed, on the one occasion when Whitman has abandoned his theory of formlessness and written in form, he has made "My Captain, O My Captain" surely one of the most tender and beautiful poems in any language.

But though Lanier elsewhere

speaks of something in Whitman which refreshed him like harsh salt spray, he was not at all disposed to accept "a great new revolutionized democratic literature, which will wear a slouch hat and have its shirt open at the bosom, and generally riot in a complete independence of form." Our civilization has never presented a more striking contrast than in these two men. In dress, in physique, in choice of service during the war, in purity as expressed in their writings, in ideals of art, of manfulness, of "democracy" they were essentially unlike. Perhaps it required the instinct of a soldier, as well as the taste of a man of letters, to perceive this contrast as clearly and to present it as trenchantly as Col. T. W. Higginson has done. "There could be little in common," says he, "between the fleshliness of 'Leaves of Grass' and the refined chivalry that could write, in 'The Symphony,' lines like these :

263

Sidney Lanier.

Shall ne'er prevail the woman's plea,
We maids would far, far whiter be
If that our eyes might sometimes see
Men maids in purity?

A man who, with pulmonary disease upon him, could still keep in his saddle as a soldier could feel but little sympathy with one who, with a superb physique prepared to serve in the hospital—honorable though that service might be for the feeble-bodied. One who viewed poetic structure as a matter of art could hardly sympathize with what he would regard as mere recitative; and one who chose his material and treatment with touch and discrimination could make no terms with one who was, as he said, 'poetry's butcher,' and offered as food only 'huge raw collops cut from the rump of poetry, and never mind gristle.''

In regard to Whitman's declaration that "meanwhile democracy waits the coming of its bards in silence and in twilight—but 'tis the twilight of dawn"—evidently having himself in mind—Lanier answers: " Professing to be a mudsill and glorying in it, chanting democracy and the shirt sleeves and equal rights, declaring that he is nothing if not one of the people; nevertheless the people, the democracy, will yet have nothing to do with him, and it is safe to say that his sole audience has lain among such representatives of the highest culture as Emerson and the English *illuminated*. The truth is, that if closely examined, Whitman, instead of being a true democrat, is simply the most incorrigible of aristocrats masking in a peasant's costume; and his poetry, instead of being the natural outcome of a fresh young democracy, is a product which would be impossible except in a highly civilized society." Lanier has no patience with Whitman's standard of "democracy." "As near as I can make it out," he writes, " Whitman's

argument seems to be that, because
a prairie is wide, therefore debauchery is admirable, and because the
Mississippi is long, therefore every
American is God." Over against
Whitman's "roughs" he sets
"George Washington, that beautiful, broad, tranquil spirit," "our
courtly and philosophic Thomas Jef-
ferson," "the Adamses and Benja-
min Franklin," "William Cullen
Bryant (that surely unrugged and
graceful figure who was so often
called the finest American gentleman) and Lowell and Longfellow;"
and in contrast with Whitman's
"rude muscle," "brawn" and "sinew of the Western backwoodsman"
as the ideal of strength, he presents
this exquisite picture: "I know—
and count it among the privileges
of my life that I do—a woman who
has spent her whole life in bed for
twenty years past, confined by a curious form of spinal disease, which
prevents locomotion, and which, in

spite of constant pain and disturbance, leaves the system long un-
worn. Day by day she lies helpless,
at the mercy of all those tyrannical
small needs which become so large
under such circumstances; every
meal must be brought to her, a
drink of water must be handed;
and she is not rich to command
service. Withal her nature is of the
brightest and most energetic sort.
Yet surrounded by these unspeakable pettinesses, inclosed in this cage
of contradictions, the woman has
made herself the center of an adoring circle of the brightest people;
her room is called 'Sunnyside;'
when brawny men are tired they go
to her for rest, when people in the
rudest physical health are sick of
life they go to her for the curative
virtue of her smiles. Now this
woman has not so much rude muscle in her whole body as Whitman's
man has in his little finger; she is
so fragile that long ago some one

called her 'White Flower,' and by
this name she is much known; it
costs her as much labor to press a
friend's hand as it costs Whitman's
rough to fell a tree; regarded from
the point of view of brawn and
sinew, she is simply absurd; yet to
the eye of my spirit there is more
manfulness in one moment of her
loving and self-sacrificing existence
than in an eon of muscle-growth
and sinew-breeding; and hers is the
manfulness which is the only solution of a true democrat, hers is the
manfulness of which only can a republic be built. A republic is the
government of the spirit; a republic
depends upon the self-control of
each member; you cannot make a
republic out of muscles and prairies
and Rocky Mountains; republics
are made of the spirit."

A mere glance at Sidney Lanier's
prose serves to show that he was "a
man of genius with a rare gift
for the happy word." But our

Sidney Lanier.

chief interest in him arises from his determination to "be in life and utterance a great poet." His life was a beautiful and inspiring poem. Was he also as a worker in the sphere of imagination and in the realm of beauty the artist—in conception and in expression the poet? Were his scientific attainments and philosophic power used to enhance and ennoble his poetic gifts, or to mar and embarrass them? Did he possess the supreme gift? For the genuine lover of poetry is firmly persuaded that no profundity, no learning can give beauty to verses that lack the divine fire. No poet in the last forty years has so puzzled the critics. Superficial as well as essential resemblances have been abundantly suggested. Lanier has been likened in moral earnestness and loftiness of purpose to Milton, in intellectuality to Emerson, in spirituality to Ruskin, in love of nature to Wordsworth, in taste, sensibility, and ex-

269

quisite sense of beauty to Shelley and Keats, in technique to Tennyson, in the astonishing manipulation of his meter and cadence and involution to Swinburne. But these comparisons, especially in their cumulative effect, are deceptive and misleading, though they serve to show, coming as they do from so many sources, that he is an original and individual singer with many rare and attractive qualities.

In his "Poems" three stages of development are discernible. In the earlier portion of his life, before 1874, music seems to have satisfied his deepest longings and highest aspirations, and in music his genius found easiest and most natural expression. As poetry was only a tangent into which he shot sometimes, there is a perceptible intellectual effort, as of one singing from the head and not out of the heart, which resulted in rigid, if not labored, movement and over-

wrought fancy. There is, at any
rate, a lack of that ease and spontaneity which was his musical birthright, and which belongs to the
poets who lisp in numbers. Of this
earlier period three poems rise distinctly above all his other efforts—
two songs for " The Jacquerie," that
of the hound and the " Betrayal,"
and " The Ship of Earth," though
there are beautiful stanzas here and
there in others, two in " Life and
Song" being specially fine. In the
first song, an allegory intended to
represent the essence of the French
revolutionary spirit growing out of
the desperate misery and the brute
force of mediæval times, though the
art is more plastic than in most of
his earlier verse, the fancy is plainly
constrained :

The hound was cuffed, the hound was
    kicked,
O' the ears was cropped, o' the tail was
    nicked,
        Oo-hoo-o, howled the hound.
The hound into his kennel crept;

Sidney Lanier.

He rarely wept, he never slept.
His mouth he always open kept,
   Licking his bitter wound,
     The hound,
     U-lu-lo, howled the hound.

A star upon his kennel shone
That showed the hound a meat-bare bone.
   O hungry was the hound!
The hound had but a churlish wit.
He seized the bone, he crunched, he bit.
"An thou wert Master, I had slit
   Thy throat with a huge wound."
     Quo' hound,
     O, angry was the hound.

The star in castle-window shone,
The Master lay abed, alone.
   O ho, why not? quo' hound.
He leapt, he seized the throat, he tore
The Master, head from neck, to floor,
And rolled the head i' the kennel door,
   And fled and salved his wound.
     Good hound!
     U-lu-lo, howled the hound.

In the "Betrayal" he is freer,
more natural, and his fancy is less
violent—more chastened, as befits
the theme. In simplicity, directness, reserved force it is strong,
though somehow it lacks the melody

272

and pathos, as well as that human
touch which goes straight to the
heart in " The Bridge of Sighs."

The sun has kissed the violet sea,
　　And burned the violet to a rose.
O sea! would thou not better be
　　Mere violet still?　Who knows? who
　　　knows?
Well hides the violet in the wood:
The dead leaf wrinkles her a hood,
And winter's ill is violet's good;
But the bold glory of the rose,
It quickly comes and quickly goes—
Red petals whirling in white snows,
　　　　Ah me!

The sun has burnt the rose-red sea:
　　The rose is turned to ashes gray.
O sea, O sea, mightst thou but be
　　The violet thou hast been to-day!
The sun is brave, the sun is bright,
The sun is lord of love and light;
But after him it cometh night.
Dim anguish of the lonesome dark!—
Once a girl's body, stiff and stark,
Was laid in a tomb without a mark,
　　　　Ah me!

" The Ship of Earth" is perhaps
not so perfect as either of the songs;
it may give evidence of the straining

ambition of youth; and yet it is the most powerful description of a young man's terror of life, in the "storm and stress" period, I remember to have seen. It suggests two strong and rugged poets, Whitman and Browning, though Lanier's was a masterful nature, too, for all its purity and love of beauty:

Thou Ship of Earth, with Death, and Birth, and Life, and Sex aboard,
And fires of Desires burning hotly in the hold,
I fear thee, O! I fear thee, for I hear the tongue and sword
At battle on the deck, and the wild mutineers are bold!

The dewdrop morn may fall from off the petal of the sky,
But all the deck is wet with blood and stains the crystal red.
A pilot, God, a pilot! for the helm is left awry,
And the best sailors in the Ship lie there among the dead!

But Lanier's was a strong and affluent nature, only less richly endowed with poetic than with musical gifts, and shortly after his removal to Baltimore he began to evince a greater mastery of the poetic art. There was observable a quick and positive gain both in poetic conception and expression. "Industrious and select reading, steady observation and insight into all seemly and generous acts and affairs," strengthened doubtless "by devout prayer to that Eternal Spirit who can enrich with all utterance and knowledge," greatly enlarged the man and fortified his resolution. Using yet the methods of the older poets, he enriched our literature with such genuine, original, and individual poems as "My Springs," "The Song of the Chattahoochee," "The Revenge of Hamish," "A Ballad of the Trees and the Master," "The Stirrup Cup," "Tampa Robins," etc., and the delightful sonnets, "The Mocking Bird," "Laus Mariæ," "A Harlequin of

Dreams," etc. Seldom did he produce so perfect a piece of work as "The Song of the Chattahoochee." In "My Springs," which is altogether a finer poem, "there is here and there a hint of the desire to say in a striking way what would best have been said in a subdued way," as the *Spectator* has said; "and again we cannot say that we like at all the

> high glory-loves
> And science-loves and story-loves.

But nothing could be more perfect than

> the whole sweet round
> Of littles that large life compound;

and the touch of wonder in the last two lines of the poem is as simple and exquisite as any touch of tenderness in our literature."

But simpler and more spontaneous is the "Song of the Chattahoochee," with its descriptive beauty and on-swaying rush, and highly musical withal—not with the baby-bustle of the eager little brook which chatters, chatters as it flows to join the brimming river, but with the more stately harmony of the manly river which is fain for to water the plain, to toil and to be mixed with main. Popular ballads, it is true, rarely touch the highest point of poetic achievement, but their very freedom and directness, the way in which they can be called up at will by the lively imagination of people not given to meditation and introspection, compensate for all a more elaborate art can supply, though no one can complain of a lack of art in this bewitching stream-song :

Out of the hills of Habersham,
Down the valleys of Hall,
I hurry amain to reach the plain,
Run the rapid and reach the fall,
Split at the rock and together again,
Accept my bed, or narrow or wide,
And flee from folly on every side

Sidney Lanier.

With a lover's pain to attain the plain
    Far from the hills of Habersham,
    Far from the valleys of Hall.

    All down the hills of Habersham,
    All through the valleys of Hall,
The rushes cried *Abide, abide,*
The willful water weeds held me thrall,
The loving laurel turned my tide,
The ferns and the fondling grass said,
    Stay,
The dewberry dipped for to work delay,
And the little reeds cried *Abide, abide,*
    Here in the hills of Habersham,
    Here in the valleys of Hall.

  .   .   .   .

    But oh, not the hills of Habersham,
    And oh, not the valleys of Hall
Avail: I am fain for to water the plain.
Downward the voices of duty call—
Downward to toil and be mixed with the
    main,
The dry fields burn, and the mills are to
    turn,
And a myriad flowers mortally yearn,
And the lordly main from beyond the
    plain
    Calls o'er the hills of Habersham,
    Calls through the valleys of Hall.

The mystical yearning and sense

of duty in this poetic interpretation
of the voices of nature are intensified to a mystic exaltation of the
power of poetic sympathy in " The
Ballad of the Trees and the Master : "

Into the woods my Master went,
Clean forspent, forspent.
Into the woods my Master came,
Forspent with love and shame.
But the olives they were not blind to
          him,
The little gray leaves were kind to him:
The thorn tree had a mind to him,
     When into the woods he came.

Out of the woods my master went,
And he was well content.
Out of the woods my Master came,
Content with death and shame.
When death and shame would woo him
          last,
From under the trees they drew him—
          last:
'Twas on a tree they slew him—last
     When out of the woods he came.

Lanier is a versatile poet in both
manner and thought, and likes to

Sidney Lanier.

give variety to his song. His
originality does not bind him to one
idea or to one form. Now he uses
nice observation, curious questioning, and quaint comparison in the
neat sonnet on "The Mocking
Bird : "

Superb and sole, upon a plumed spray
That o'er the general leafage boldly
    grew,
He summed the woods in song; or typic
    drew
The watch of hungry hawks, the lone
    dismay
Of languid doves when long their lovers
    stray,
And all birds' passion-plays that sprinkle
    dew
At morn in brake or bosky avenue.
Whate'er birds did or dreamed, this bird
    could say.
Then down he shot, bounced airily along
The sward, twitched in a grasshopper,
    made song
Midflight, perched, prinked, and to his
    art again.
Sweet Science, this large riddle read me
    plain:
How may the death of that dull insect be
280

Sidney Lanier.

The life of yon trim Shakspere on the
    tree?

  ᐱThen again in the same verse form
he gives his luxuriant fancy freer
play and takes us into the higher region of the imagination in " The
Harlequin of Dreams : "

Swift, through some trap mine eyes
    have never found,
Dim-paneled in the painted scene of
    Sleep,
Thou, giant Harlequin of Dreams, dost
    leap
Upon my spirit's stage. Then Sight and
    Sound,
Then Space and Time, then Language,
    Mete and Bound,
And all familiar Forms that firmly keep
Man's reason in the road, change faces,
    peep
Betwixt the legs and mock the daily
    round.
Yet thou canst more than mock: some-
    times my tears
At midnight break through bounden
    lids—a sign
Thou hast a heart: and oft thy little
    leaven

Sidney Lanier.

Of dream-taught wisdom works me bet-
tered years.
In one night witch, saint, trickster, fool
divine,
I think thou'rt jester at the Court of
Heaven.

In the third stage of Lanier's poetical development, however, the
most distinctive features of his art
and gifts are presented. According
to his own theories were written
those poems in which he gave the
best exhibition of his melody,
strength, and personal flavor, and
the highest manifestation of his passion, power, and originality. In
these his luxuriant fancy has freest
range; his love of nature is most
poetically displayed. In these later
poems we may, it is true, still chance
upon a line fashioned after Poe and
observe a manner imitated from
Browning, for not even "dearest
Keats," it would seem, exercised
such an influence upon him as these;
yet no other poet ever wrote a series

282

of poems like " Corn," " Clover," " The Bee," " Remonstrance," " The Crystal," " The Symphony," " Individuality," " Sunset," " The Marshes of Glynn," and " Sunrise." In merit most unequal, in peculiarities most marked, they are nevertheless distinctive, and they are poetry, surely the rarest product of English or American literature during the last quarter of a century. After all it is to this body of verse we must turn for the completest interpretation of Lanier's ideas of the poet, of personality, of life, nature, love, God. If it be asked, " What profit e'er a poet brings? " he answers in " The Bee : "

He beareth starry stuff about his wings
To pollen thee and sting thee fertile:
.   .   .   .
       for oft these pollens be
Fine dust from wars that poets wage for
  thee.

Or, if the question be, "A poet, thou ; what worth, what worth, the

whole of all thine art?" we learn
from "Clover:"

The artist's market is the heart of man,
The artist's price, some little good of man.

In "Corn," one tall corn-captain
types

   The poet-soul sublime
That leads the vanward of his timid time
And sings up cowards with commanding
  rhyme;

addressing whom he sings:

 Thou lift'st more stature than a mortal
   man's
Yet ever piercest downward in the mold
  And keepest hold
Upon the reverend and steadfast earth
  That gave thee birth;
Yea, standest smiling in thy future grave,
  Serene and brave,
 With unremitting breath
 Inhaling life from death,
Thine epitaph writ fair in fruitage elo-
  quent,
  Thyself thy monument.

  As poets should
Thou hast built up thy hardihood
 With universal food,

Sidney Lanier.

Drawn in select proportion fair
   From honest mold and vaga-
      bond air;
From darkness of the dreadful night,
   And joyful light;
From antique ashes, whose departed
     flame
In thee has finer life and longer fame;
   From wounds and balms,
   From storms and calms,
   From potsherds and dry bones
     And ruin-stones.
Into thy vigorous substance thou hast
     wrought
Whate'er the hand of Circumstance hath
     brought;
   Yea, into cool solacing green hast
     spun
White radiance hot from out the sun.
So thou dost mutually leaven
Strength of earth with grace of heaven;
   So thou dost marry new and old
   Into a one of higher mold;
   So thou dost reconcile the hot and cold,
     The dark and bright,
   And many a perplexing opposite,
     And so,
   Akin by blood to high and low,
Fitly thou playest out thy poet's part,
Richly expending thy much-bruisèd
     heart

285

Sidney Lanier.

In equal care to nourish lord in hall
  Or beast in stall:
Thou took'st from all that thou mightest
  give to all.

The author of this conception of
a poet therefore very naturally con-
siders all the questions of the hour
and ponders the problems of the day.
To the old hill of his native state,
worn out, abandoned, he exclaims
with prophetic voice in " Corn : "

Thou gashed and hairy Lear
Whom the divine Cordelia of the year,
E'en pitying Spring, will vainly strive to
  cheer—

    .   .   .   .

Yet shall the great God turn thy fate,
And bring thee back into thy monarch
  state
  And majesty immaculate.

Against unbelief and all half-be-
liefs he protests in " Acknowledg-
ment," and " Remonstrance " contains his fierce denunciation against
bigotry and intolerance, concluding
with :

Sidney Lanier.

Opinion, damned intriguer, gray with
    guile,
  Let me alone!

The cold, metallic spirit of money-
getting—with its paralyzing effect
upon all the finer instincts and nobler passions of the soul, with its
destructive consequences to the
saint's faith, the artist's love of
beauty, and the poet's high imagin-
ings, and its accompanying degradation of the poor—afflicted him
still more deeply. In the "Symphony" he cries out:

O Trade! O Trade! would thou wert
    dead!
The time needs heart—'tis tired of head:

and the song of the poor,

Wedged by the pressing of Trade's hand,

is eloquent with melodious heart-
throbs:

We weave in the mills and heave in the
    kilns,
We sieve mine-meshes under the hills,
And thieve much gold from the devil's
    bank tills

287

Sidney Lanier.

To relieve, O God, what manner of ills?
The beasts, they hunger, and eat, and die;
And so do we, and the world's a sty;
Hush, fellow-swine: why nuzzle and
      cry?
Swinehood hath no remedy,
Say many men, and hasten by,
Clamping the nose and blinking the eye.
But who said once, in the lordly tone,
Man shall not live by bread alone,
But all that cometh from the Throne?
     Hath God said so?
     But Trade saith, *No:*
And the kilns and the curt-tongued mills
      say, *Go:*
There's plenty that can, if you can't, we
      know.
Move out, if you think you're underpaid.
The poor are prolific, we're not afraid:
     Trade is trade.

.   .   .   .

Alas, for the poor to have some part
In yon sweet living lands of art,
Makes problems not for head, but heart.
Vainly might Plato's head revolve it:
Plainly the heart of a child could solve it.

Love alone, then, can cure the
ills that flesh is heir to, can solve
the difficulties arising from so many
sources, and Lanier uses every note

288

in his gamut in sounding love's praises :

Music is love in search of a word.

And in an ecstasy of love he exclaims :

O, sweet my pretty sum of history,
I leapt the breadth of time in loving
   thee!

For " music means harmony, harmony means love, and love means—God."

I would thou left'st me free to live with
      love
   And faith, that through the love of
   love doth find
My Lord's dear presence in the stars
      above,
   The clods below, the flesh without, the
   mind
Within, the bread, the tear, the smile.

His view of life may then be given in one line :

When life's all love,' tis life : aught else,
   'tis naught.

To the lover of nature Lanier gives the keenest delight and sub-

tlest pleasure. The poet has achieved
the triumph of sharing with others
that "inward thrill in the air, or in
the sunshine, one knows not which,
half like the thrill of the passion of
love, half like the thrill of the passion of friendship" which he expe-
rienced on a "divine day." "Do
you like, as I do," he asks Paul H.
Hayne, "on such a day to go out
into the sunlight and *stop thinking ?*
—lie fallow, like a field, and absorb
those certain liberal potentialities
which will in after days reappear,
duly formulated, duly grown, duly
perfected, as poems?" Knowledge
of facts and sensibility to charms,
we have been told, are the two elements in a perfectly poetical appreciation of nature, and Lanier possessed both to an eminent degree.
In his communion with nature mind
and soul seemed to be divested of
their outer garment, so delicate was
his organism, so observant was he
of minutest particulars, so exqui-

Sidney Lanier.

sitely attuned was his ear. His
knowledge of nature was that of a
friend and lover, who was at the
same time a naturalist. But unlike
Wordsworth, from whose " noblest
utterances man is absent," says
Lowell, " except as the antithesis
that gives a sharper emphasis to
nature," man is everywhere the
central figure or controlling influence in Lanier's most beautiful nature poems. His personifications,
always bold, are often powerful,
though the affectations, " cousin
Clover," "cousin Cloud," " sweet-
heart leaves," have been greatly
overpraised. The tense imagination observable here and there also
mars their beauty and power. But
his infinite tenderness, pliancy of
fancy, and susceptibility to nature's
charms were happily combined with
the power of transporting us into the
midst of the " gospeling glooms,"
into the very presence of the marsh
and the sea. With him we can catch

291

Sidney Lanier.

The wood smells that swiftly but now
    brought breath
From the heaven-side bank of the river
    of death;

and we can feel that

The slant yellow beam down the wood
    aisle doth seem
Like a lane into heaven that leads from
    a dream.

He teaches us "to company with
large, amiable trees," and

To loiter down lone alleys of delight,
    And hear the beating of the hearts of
        trees,
And think the thoughts that lilies speak
    in white
    By greenwood pools and pleasant pas-
        sages.

And in his company, too, we may
experience the various ministrations
of nature,

    For love, the dear wood's sympathies,
    For grief, the wise wood's peace.

Nature affects him like music:

    Shaken with happiness:
    The gates of sleep stood wide.

Sidney Lanier.

For, as the opening lines of " Sunrise " inform us,

In my sleep I was fain of their fellow-
     ship, fain
Of the live oaks, the marsh, and the main.
The little green leaves would not let me
     alone in my sleep.

An oft-quoted touch of tenderness
and fancy is taken from " Corn : "

The leaves that wave against my cheek
     caress
Like women's hands ; the embracing
     bows express
A subtlety of mighty tenderness;
The copse depths into little noises start,
That sound anon like beatings of a heart,
Anon like talk 'twixt lips not far apart.

The " Hymns of the Marshes " afford abundant examples of his larger, more thoughtful manner. Peculiarly characteristic of his tolerant, worshipful nature is this :

Oh, what is abroad in the marsh and the
     terminal sea?
Somehow my soul seems suddenly free
From the weighing of fate and the sad
     discussion of sin,

Sidney Lanier.

By the length and the breadth and the
  sweep of the marshes of Glynn.

Ye marshes, how candid and simple and
  nothing-withholding and free
Ye publish yourselves to the sky and
  offer yourselves to the sea!
Tolerant plains, that suffer the sea and
  the rains and the sun,
Ye spread and span like the catholic man
  who hath mightily won
God out of knowledge and good out of
  infinite pain
And sight out of blindness and purity out
  of stain.

As the marsh hen secretly builds on the
  watery sod,
Behold, I will build me a nest on the
  greatness of God:
I will fly in the greatness of God as the
  marsh hen flies
In the freedom that fills all the space
  'twixt the marsh and the skies:
By so many roots as the marsh grass
  sends in the sod,
I will heartily lay me a-hold on the
  greatness of God:
O, like to the greatness of God is the
  greatness within
The range of the marshes, the liberal
  marshes of Glynn.

Sidney Lanier.

Lanier's poetry appeals rather to meditative minds than to those delighting in pictorial effects. "The Song of the Chattahoochee" is characteristically less picturesque than "The Brook." But in "Sunrise" Lanier presents a picture of remarkable brilliance and fascination, though it does seem "to stand on tiptoe here and there with the desire to express the inexpressible."

Oh, what if a sound should be made!
Oh, what if a bound should be laid
To this bow-and-spring tension of beauty
      and silence a-spring—
To the bend of beauty the bow, or the
      hold of silence the string!
I fear me, I fear me yon dome of diaph-
      anous gleam
Will break as a bubble o'erblown in a
      dream—
Yon dome of too-tenuous tissues of space
      and of night.
Overweighted with stars, overfreighted
      with light,
Oversated with beauty and silence, will
      seem
But a bubble that broke in a dream,

If a bound of degree to this grace be
  laid,
Or a sound or a motion made.

But no: it is made: list! Somewhere—
  mystery, where?
     In the leaves? in the air?
In my heart? is a motion made:
'Tis a motion of dawn, like a flicker of
  shade on shade.
In the leaves 'tis palpable: low multitu-
  dinous stirring
Upwinds through the woods; the little
  ones, softly conferring,
Have settled my lord's to be looked for;
  so; they are still;
But the air and my heart and the earth
  are a-thrill—
And look where the wild duck sails round
  the bend of the river—
And look where a passionate shiver
Expectant is bending the blades
Of the marsh grass in serial shimmers
  and shades—
And invisible wings, fast fleeting, fast
  fleeting,
     Are beating
The dark overhead as my heart beats—
  and steady and free
Is the ebb tide flowing from marsh to sea—
  (Run home, little streams,

With your lapfuls of stars and
    dreams)—
And a sailor unseen is hoisting a-peak,
For list, down the inshore curve of the
    creek
How merrily flutters the sail—
And lo! in the East! Will the East un-
    veil?
The East is unveiled, the East hath con-
    fessed
A flush: 'tis dead; 'tis alive; 'tis dead ere
    the West
Was aware of it: nay, 'tis abiding, 'tis
    unwithdrawn:
Have a care, sweet Heaven! 'Tis Dawn!

Lanier felt in his innermost heart
that—

How dark, how dark soever the race that
    must needs be run,
I am lit with the sun.

With enkindled gaze and calmly
unafraid he therefore sings his life
song on the very brink of the grave:

Oh, never the mast-high run of the seas
      Of traffic shall hide thee,
Never the hell-covered smoke of the fac-
    tories
      Hide thee,

Sidney Lanier.

Never the reek of the time's fen-politics
    Hide thee,
And ever my heart through the night
    shall with knowledge abide thee,
And ever by day shall my spirit, as one
    that hath tried thee,
Labor, at leisure, in art—till yonder be-
    side thee
My soul shall float, friend Sun,
The day being done.

George W. Cable.

IN the far South lies a region unique in its climate, its scenery, and its civilization. It comprises about one-half (the Southern portion) of the state of Louisiana, and is known as the land of the Creoles. The soft, luxurious climate is said to be enervating, but though its languid airs have induced a certain softness of utterance in the speech of the inhabitants, they have lost little of the old Gallic alertness, intrepidity, and strength of body and mind; for this civilization was born of purely French enterprise, modified somewhat by Spanish association and control, but steadily impervious to English influences. The American brought this region into the family of states, but he himself was stopped upon the threshold of its

inner life and admitted to the
charmed circle only upon the acceptance of the manners and ideas
of the Creoles; for your Creole is
the lineal descendant of the Frenchman that gave one of those quick
answers for which his countrymen
have long been proverbial. "If I
were not an Englishman," said the
gracious islander, "I would choose
next to be a Frenchman." "Yes,
sir, and if I were not a Frenchman,
I would choose next to be a Frenchman."

Their country is a land of bay-
ous, lakes, swamps, and rich, large
plantations. On the banks of these
natural dikes and sluices are to be
seen the dense, weirdly beautiful,
semitropical forests skirting the
broad fields of cotton, of corn, of
rice, and of cane, which open out
into an almost illimitable expanse
and lie basking and ripening in the
sun of a long and dazzlingly beautiful summer. An evening scene in
300

George W. Cable.

this land which Mr. Cable has so
vividly painted suggests an ideal
background for romance and poetry.
"In the last hours of the day those
scenes are often illuminated with an
extraordinary splendor. From the
boughs of the dark, broad-spreading
live-oak, and the phantom-like arms
of the lofty cypresses, the long,
motionless pendants of pale gray
moss point down to their inverted
images in the unruffled waters beneath them. Nothing breaks the
wide-spread silence. The light of
the declining sun at one moment
brightens the tops of the cypresses,
at another glows like a furnace behind their black branches, or, as the
voyager reaches a western turn of
the bayou, swings slowly round,
and broadens down in dazzling
crimson and purple upon the mirror of the stream. Now and then,
from out some hazy shadow, a
heron, white or blue, takes silent
flight; an alligator crossing the

stream sends out long, tinted bars
of widening ripple; or on some
high, fire-blackened tree a flock of
roosting vultures, silhouetted on the
sky, linger with half-opened, un-
willing wing, and flap away by
ones and twos until the tree is bare.
Should the traveler descry, first
as a mote intensely black in the
midst of the brilliancy that over-
spreads the water, and by and by
revealing itself in true outline and
proportion as a small canoe containing two men, whose weight
seems about to engulf it, and by
whose paddle-strokes it is impelled
with such evenness and speed that
a long, glassy wave gleams continually at either side a full inch higher than the edge of the boat, he
will have before him a picture of
nature and human life that might
have been seen at any time since
the French fathers of the Louisiana
Creoles colonized the Delta."

But the Creoles, like all of the

George W. Cable.

French race, are seen to best advantage in the city. By nature or long
habit they have become adapted to
society, and in their city of New
Orleans built up a lesser Paris, which
the latest and most delightful historian of the Creole capital says
should be personified as the most
feminine of women. Her good
qualities and her defects, her tem-
pers and furies, her gaiety and her
pleasure-loving disposition, her peculiar delicacy and refinement, her
strength and nobility in sorrow and
misfortune — her whole character
was brought entire from France.
Charming she is, of course, and
also individual and interesting, " an
enigma to prudes and a paradox to
Puritans." Nature, too, is feminine,
and it would seem that she was in
one of her most paradoxical moods
when George W. Cable was born
in the Creoles' city, October 12,
1844.

On his father's side he was de-

George W. Cable.

scended from an old colonial family
of Virginia, the Cabells, whose
name was originally spelled Cable,
their ancient coat of arms introduc-
ing the cable as an accessory; but
either owing to the early death of
his father or for some other cause
Mr. Cable has not exhibited any of
the special traits of his Virginian
ancestry. The old New England
stock represented in his mother
has seemed to constitute the warp
and woof of his nature, though it
has been not a little influenced by
association with his Gallic neighbors. His father and mother met
in Indiana, where they were married in 1834, and after the financial
crash of 1837 they sought their
fortune in New Orleans. For a
time the father prospered in business; then came misfortune, and
after a second disastrous failure, in
1859, he died, leaving the family
in straitened circumstances. The
fourteen-year-old boy was taken

from his studies, just as he was about to graduate from the high school, and put to clerking, that he might help in the support of the household. At this occupation he remained till 1863, when his sisters were sent beyond the Federal lines for refusing to take the oath of allegiance : and such was his youthful appearance and diminutive stature that they had no trouble in taking their "little brother" with them. He entered the Confederate army at once, and served to the close of the war in Gen. Wirt Adams's brigade of Mississippians. One incident of his campaigning has furnished material for an amusing story, which the delightful raconteur tells with much humor. The company to which he belonged had for hours been on an exciting chase after a band of Federal raiders, who were laying waste the plantations south of the Red River. "At one time the hot pur-

George W. Cable.

suit promised immediate success.
The Yankees were at Mr. ——'s
plantation. Over the ditches,
through the cane fields the Confederate cavalry spurred their panting
horses to fresh effort. Again too
late! The planter stood under a
live-oak on his trampled lawn, ga-
zing with an air of bewilderment at
a raw-boned, blind, broken-winded
horse, upon which was seated an
old gray-headed negro, who blankly
returned his master's expressionless
stare. This equestrian statue of
ruin was quickly surrounded by
eager avengers. The officer in
command questioned the planter as
to the number and probable route
of the enemy. Mr. —— only
shook his head mournfully, repeating in a mechanical manner an enu-
meration of his losses, ending with,
'Not a horse or a hoof left, except
that broken-winded old racer,' and
the index-finger pointed fixedly at
the blindly blinking eyes of the mo-

George W. Cable.

tionless animal. Fresh questioning
brought the same answer, with its
pitiful refrain, 'Only that broken-
winded old racer,' until the planter
caught sight of Cable. His eyes
seemed magnetically fastened, and
his voice fell to an abysmal depth,
as he asked : 'My son, do *you* belong to the army?' 'Come on,'
called the captain, 'Mr. ——'s
losses have upset his mind.' Down
the avenue of live-oak, over the
broken fences, filed the cavalry,
closing the ranks as they crossed
the ditch and got up in the dirt
road, urging on their tired horses
with hand and spur, till a lagging
soldier called : 'Here comes Mr.
—— after us, on the old racer.
He's waked the old hoss up, and
they're a booming along like a
steam-injine. Maybe he's come to
himself and is going to tell us whar
we can ketch the Yankees.' Gallantly came the racer, breaking into
the ranks like a thunderbolt, and
307

scattering the cavalry to right and left, until, tugging at the reins, the rider succeeded in stopping him beside Cable. There was a husky, grieved tone in his voice as he repeated his former question: 'My little son, do *you* belong to the army?' Proudly the youth raised himself in his stirrups, straightening out the last quarter of an inch of his height; then bowed assent. The planter dropped his reins, threw up his arms and with a despairing look exclaimed: 'Great heavens! Abe Lincoln told the truth. We *are* robbing the cradle and the grave!'"

From early childhood Mr. Cable had been studious, and his studious habits he took with him into the army. His leisure hours were given to the study of the Bible, to keeping up his knowledge of Latin grammar, and working out problems of higher mathematics. The hardships and stirring scenes of camp and army life quickly changed the raw recruit into a thoughtful young man ; and he is described as having been a good soldier, scrupulously observant of discipline, always at his post and always courageous and daring. From a dangerous wound in the left armpit he barely escaped with his life.

At the close of the war Mr. Cable, like most of his comrades, was without a dollar. Returning to New Orleans, he became errand boy, then clerked for six months in Kosciusko, Miss., after which he returned again to New Orleans, studied civil engineering, and joined a surveying company sent by the state into the Têche country to establish the lines and levels along the banks of the Achafalaya River. An attack of malarial fever followed, from which he did not fully recover for two years. Going back to the bookkeeper's desk again, he shortly began to rise, becoming first sec-

George W. Cable.

retary to a company for the manu-
facture of cottonseed oil, and then
accountant and cashier of William
C. Black & Co., cotton factors.
While holding the latter position he
acted also as secretary to the treas-
urer of the New Orleans Cotton
Exchange and to its Finance Committee. But though engaged in
business, Mr. Cable was assiduous-
ly acquiring a liberal education, and
developing more and more an eager
interest in general culture and public matters. In this way he became a contributor to a special column in the *Picayune*, over the sig-
nature of "Drop-Shot," and had
his first experience in writing. The
contributions were critical and humorous papers, with an occasional
bit of verse, and appeared only once
a week; but in a little while he was
attached to the staff, and they became a daily feature of the paper.
In a chatty manner Mr. Cable has
told of the natural way in which he

310

George W. Cable.

drifted into literature in an interview
published in the *Picayune:*

What kind of work did I do? That's
a question, and there's where the trouble
comes in. There was no such a thing as
a division of labor in those days, and
each man had to do anything and everything that might turn up. I had stipu-
lated at first not to do certain kinds of
reporting, and this didn't please the old
man very well. It was one of his rules
that each man should do whatever was
required of him, and I became rather in
the way. Then I wanted to be always
writing, and they wanted me to be always reporting. This didn't work well,
and so when the summer came on, and
they began to reduce expenses, it was intimated to me that my resignation would
be accepted. I vowed that I would never
have anything to do with a newspaper
again, and I went back to bookkeeping.
I was in a large cotton house, and I kept
their accounts for a while, until I finally
offered to take entire charge of the
counting-room at so much salary per
year, and hire what assistance I wanted.
This suited the firm as well as it did me,
and I began to do more and more literary
work. Finally I employed a cashier, and

George W. Cable.

all day I would write at my desk, only
being consulted by him on important
matters. I was making a beginning
then. I first carried on a weekly column
in the *Picayune;* but it wasn't very pleasant to work for a paper managed by a
board of directors, and at last I quit it.
This writing of trifles after a while grew
wearisome, and I resolved to put it into
stories.

The stipulation was in regard to
the theater, we have been told; and
when it was considered necessary
to give him charge of the theatrical
column he positively refused to do
the work.

It was the fascinating episodes of
early New Orleans life which again
tempted him to use his pen, and
which now in their artistic setting
of short stories turned all eyes upon
the writer and his native city. Three
of these had been written at odd moments in the midst of clerical duties, when the old *Scribner's Monthly*, now the *Century Magazine*,
sent a commission to New Orleans

312

to write and illustrate the " Great
South Papers."   At Mr. Cable's re-
quest a member of this commission,
Mr. Edward King, sent one of the
stories to the magazine, and though
it was returned, a second venture
" was not only successful, but called
forth a sympathetic and inspiring
letter from Richard Watson Gilder,
the young associate editor to Dr.
Holland."   " Sieur George " it was
called, and the very first words
were significant : " In the heart of
New Orleans."   " Belles Demoi-
selles Plantation," " Tite Poulette,"
" Jean-ah Poquelin," " Madame Dé-
licieuse," and " Café des Exilés,"
now appeared at intervals covering
about two years in all, and then
with the inimitable " Posson Jone,"
which appeared in *Appleton's Journal*, were issued in a single volume
under the title of " Old Creole
Days" (1879).   These stories made a
twofold revelation : a new field of
romance, rich in the contrasts and

colors of an old, unique, and varied civilization, steeped in sentiment and passion, and enveloped in the poetic, many-tinted haze of a semitropical clime; and also the master hand of a literary artist, who, to the moral energy and sinewy fiber of English character, added the grace, delicacy, airy lightness, and excitability of the Latin race. They also showed that the author was a born story-teller.

In this first volume there are no suggestions of the amateur, nothing crude, unfinished. The pictures of life are as exquisitely clear as they are delicately tender or tragically sorrowful. Arch humor and playful fancy throw a bright ray into scenes of pure pathos, or give a joyous note to the tender tones of happy loves, which would otherwise grow monotonous; but in the tragic story of "Jean-ah Poquelin" the slow martyrdom is painted in gloomy shadows, and the pathos, imagery, and dramatic force of this sketch first suggested comparison with Hawthorne. These stories are all good, but " Posson Jone " is the masterpiece of the collection. In Jules St. Ange, a perfect creation in miniature, Mr. Cable has so thoroughly caught the very spirit of the French race that it would seem downright rude and coarse to apply matter-of-fact English words and standards of morals and conduct to the gay, pleasure-loving, kindhearted, volatile little Creole. With rare skill, too, does the author cast the idealizing light of genius upon the awkward backwoods preacher, the street, the drinking-place, the vulgar confidence game, the gambling-saloon, the bull-ring and motley crew of spectators, the calaboose, the departing boat, the returning prodigal, which lifts them forever out of the realm of the sordid and the commonplace into that of pure art and abiding beauty. This ele-

gant little heathen is as much a
monument to the author's heart as
it is to his dramatic skill.

At the accountant's desk two
more years were spent without further literary activity. But even
during the period of convalescence
from malarial fever the young man
had eagerly applied himself to the
study of natural history, and laid
the foundation for those beautiful
pictures of swamp, bayou, prairie,
and still life, which are such marked
features of his writings, in exact
scientific knowledge as well as in
close observation. So at this time,
and later, Mr. Cable extended his
studies and researches into the
speech, songs, manners, customs,
personal traits, and characteristics of
the Creoles, covering their entire
history from the earliest settlements
in Louisiana to the present time.
Thus equipped, he was ready to
give immediate attention to the re-
quest of the *Century Magazine*

for a twelve months' serial. The result was " The Grandissimes." Before him lay the story of " Bras Coupé," which had been offered for publication as a short story and rejected, and this now became the central idea of a genuine romance of Louisiana at the beginning of this century. Over the differences of race, the bitterness of caste prejudice, restiveness under imposed rule, jealousy of the alien ruler, and suspicion of the newcomer, which largely constituted the situation at that time, was cast the warm coloring of a poetic imagination. But a note struck only here and there in the short stories now becomes the theme of all Mr. Cable's writings. It did not occur to him, it would seem, that an artist out of his domain is not infrequently the least clear-sighted of mortals; that the poet, if he is to be our only truth-teller, must let politics alone. But to this Mr. Cable has answered, " For all he was the farthest remove from a mere party contestant or spoilsman, neither his righteous pugnacity nor his human sympathy would allow him to ' let politics alone ; ' " for he doubtless had himself in mind when he wrote these words in regard to Dr. Sevier. Indeed, he belongs to the class of thoroughgoing men, actuated by thoroughgoing logic, lovers of abstract truth and perfect ideals, and it was his lot to be born among a people who by the necessities of their situation were controlled by practical expediency. They were compelled to adopt an illogical but practical compromise between two extremes which were logical but not practical. This conflict between theory and actuality, of abstract truth with practical expedience, has so affected the sensitive nature of an extremely artistic temperament as to make this writer give a prejudiced, incorrect, unjust picture of Southern life, char-

acter, and situation. This domina-
tion of one idea has vitiated the
most exquisite literary and artistic
gifts that any American writer of
fiction, with possibly one exception,
has been endowed with since Hawthorne, though in respect to intellectuality, to imagination, to profound insight into life, to a full,
rich, large, and true humanity, one
would be overbold to institute comparison between him and America's
greatest writer.

Both the time and Mr. Cable's
methods, now that of the ardent
controversialist espousing the ex-
tremest measures of partisan politics, and again that of the consummate artist holding up a people to
the scorn and detestation of the
world, were unsuited either to a phil-
anthrophic and benevolent, or to a
true artistic handling of this theme.
The Southerners were suffering
from the desolations of a devasta-
ting war and the humiliating expe-

riences of " reconstruction." Under
these adverse and almost blinding
conditions many of them felt the
call of duty to deal righteously with
the most difficult problem any people has ever been called upon to
work out. But time and the practical common sense of the American
people have made it possible to give
to this question the solution of a slow,
patient, and orderly growth. We
are now concerned only with tracing
the effect produced upon the writer
by this protracted struggle between
the artist and the man with a mission,
which began in " The Grandissimes"
and was completed in " John March
Southerner."

In " The Grandissimes " (1880)
Mr. Cable has forsaken the beaten
track of character study with its
brilliant, indefinite conversations and
subtle moral and intellectual problems, and returned to the old romance. Yet he is modern, and has
taken with him into the older field

George W. Cable.

an artist's nice eye for color and
the picturesque, an artist's fine sense
of workmanship, and an artist's aim
of producing effect in a natural way
and by dramatic skill. The story
itself is interesting. The Grandissimes and the De Grapions emerge
from the haze of a romantic past
into the actual present with the
reader's keenest interest aroused in
their fortunes, their feud, the ancient and honorable character of
their ancestry, and their pride and
family feeling. With t h e first
Grandissime came a Fusilier, who
married an Indian princess; and
when the Grandissimes became so
many as the sands of the Mississippi innumerable, "in every flock
might always be seen a Fusilier or
two, fierce - eyed, strong - beaked,
dark, heavy-taloned birds, who, if
they could not sing, were of rich
plumage, and could talk and bite
and strike." To this wide connection and powerful family influence

the De Grapions offer a pathetic
contrast. "Though they were brilliant, gallant, much loved, early
epauleted fellows," they had a sad
aptness for dying young. "A lone
son following a lone son, and he
another," the family dwindles till
only two women are left. One of
these marries the head of the
Grandissimes, and the other, her
daughter, a German, and the De
Grapion name passes away. The
hero and heroine, Honoré Grandissime and Aurora De Grapion, who
unite at last the fortunes of the two
families, are the author's best por-
traits of higher Creole life. Aurora, in naturalness and finish, is as
much a creation of genius as Jules
St. Ange, Raoul, Narcisse—a kind
of characterization in which he ex-
cels. In the delineation of a gentleman, Honoré and Dr. Sevier for examples, this author succeeds about
as well as most writers of fiction—
that is, very poorly. A few realistic

touches, at best a type, is as a rule the
most that we may expect. Palmyre
and Agricola, however, each in a
very different way, offered a rare
opportunity for individual, powerful
characterization, but the dominant
theme would only admit of their
use to point a moral and adorn a
tale. Clotilde and Frowenfeld are
lay figures, for, with the exception
of Aurora and Raoul, "it may be
said of the story, as the author remarks of a narrative of one of his
characters: 'There shone a light of
romance upon it that filled it with
color and populated it with phantoms.'"

The theme of "The Grandissimes" is the effect produced upon
a tropical society by an institution
which deprives a human being of
his liberty, gives rise to a feeling of
caste, and the maintenance of which
involves a separation in thought and
feeling from the rest of the civilized
world. In the portion of the South

in which Mr. Cable was reared
slavery had fewer mitigating circumstances than in any other; and he
seems to have approached the study
of the question from the point of view
of the French Revolution and with
the philosophy of Rousseau. The
latter is the basis of the Bras Coupé
story. Over the entire romance, over
action and incident and scene and
character, hangs the pall of slavery,
with just enough light and color introduced to deepen the shadows.
The effect upon the individual and
society is brought out admirably,
now by skilful word-painting and
again by still more skilful dramatic
action. But too frequently the author throws his puppets aside and
appears in person upon the scene.
The man with a mission throttles
the artist. At such times he makes
sententious comments or utters commonplaces now universally accepted, and still more frequently he indulges in sharp thrusts and biting

sarcasms—all from the point of view of art not only blemishes, but "palpable intrusions." A few out of some thirty, forty, fifty, a hundred, in " The Grandissimes " will illustrate this point : " Those Creoles have such a shocking way of filing their family relics and records in ratholes." " One American trait which the Creole is never entirely ready to encounter is this gratuitous Yankee way of going straight to the root of things." " For, blow the wind east or blow the wind west, the affinity of the average Grandissime for a salary abideth forever." " The playful, mock-martial tread of the delicate Creole feet is all at once swallowed by the sound of many heavier steps in the hall, and the fathers, grandfathers, sons, brothers, uncles, and nephews of the great family come out, not a man of them that cannot, with a little care, keep on his feet." " No power or circimstance has ever been found that

will keep a Creole from talking."
"You may see their grandchildren
to-day, anywhere within the angle
of the rues Esplanade and Rampart,
holding up their heads in unspeakable poverty, their nobility kept
green by unflinching self-respect,
and their poetic and pathetic pride
reveling in ancestral, perennial re-
bellion against common sense."
The abundance of such remarks in
Mr. Cable's writings may perhaps
account for the Creoles' peculiar affection for him. "Like all other
luxuries, the perpetration of an epi-
gram has to be paid for."

Mr. Brander Matthews has drawn
a nice distinction between humor
and the sense of humor, observing
that the ownership of one does not
insure possession of the other.
"Probably," he adds, "if the sense
of humor had been more acutely developed in Dickens, he might even
have refrained from out-heroding
Herod in his massacre of the inno-

cents." But in some authors the love of melodrama is too deeply planted to be uprooted. A sense of humor equal to this author's rich gift of humor would have been required to save our nerves from the tragico-sentimental story of Bras Coupé, the wanton murder of Clemence and the revolting death of the pot-hunter in the beautiful idyl of "Bonaventure." In at least two of these instances his nice artistic sensibility has been dulled by partisan feeling. Partisanship of any kind implies a more or less one-sided view. Was Shakespeare's impartiality in regard to religion and government attributable to indifference or to the artist's affinities for the essential rather than the phenomenal, for t h e permanent rather than the conventional? "The old play," a scholar tells us in writing of King John, "was written in the service of the Reformation, the reign of King John affording abun-

dance of material when molded by
a strong partisan spirit (which the
author, whoever he was, certainly
had) for emphasizing what he regarded as the evils of papal rule,
and its antagonism to a vital nationality. Its violent partisan spirit,
though entirely inconsistent with a
true artistic spirit, and its appeals
to the vulgar antagonisms of the
groundlings, must have secured for
it a great popularity at the time
when it first appeared. Of this
violent partisan spirit there's not a
trace in Shakespeare's play."

In " Madame Delphine " (1881)
we see the most perfect specimen of
the author's literary art and con-
structive ability. The story is so
quickly told and so skilfully handled
as almost to leave us unaware of
the utter improbability of the plot.
The narrative glides as smoothly as
a brook " purling down with silver
waves." While the compass does not
admit of the exhibition of strength

George W. Cable.

shown in "The Grandissimes," it also prevents the digressions and extravagances which mar that romance. The setting of this exquisite gem is perfect. "A beautiful summer night, when all nature seemed hushed in ecstacy, one of those Southern nights under whose spell all the sterner energies of the mind cloak themselves and lie down in bivouac, and the fancy and the imagination, that cannot sleep, slip their fetters and escape, beckoned away from behind every flowering bush and sweet-smelling tree, and every stretch of lonely, half-lighted walk, by the genius of poetry. The air stirred softly now and then, and was still again, as if the breezes lifted their expectant pinions and lowered them once more, awaiting the rising of the moon in a silence which fell upon the field, the roads, the gardens, the walls, and the suburban and half-suburban streets, like a pause in worship." The

329

---

dark boughs of the orange tree, the first low flute notes of the mocking-bird's all-night song, the overpowering sweetness of the night jasmine, the old gate with the grass growing about it in a thick turf, as though the entrance had not been used for years ; the dilapidated garden fence and house, as significant of the fortunes of its inmates ; the wider view of the city and its atmosphere —form an ideal frame-work for the lifelike portrait of Madame Delphine. And the little priest with his big heart and rare sermon is also a living character exactly adapted to his surroundings. But the other characters are merely introduced for the sake of the theme. If the author had been content to leave this charming story as a fairy tale for quadroons, we might have given to it that unalloyed enjoyment which is so easily accorded to those delightful creations of the fancy. But instead it has rather suited his purpose to burden his art with an ethical teaching which does not bear close scrutiny. When the pirate Lemaitre opens a bank, presumably with his ill-gotten gains, makes provision to elude the officers of the law, and is nevertheless called by God's priest " God's own banker," we turn with infinite relief to an artist who had no sentimentality, and whose sentiment never obscured either his artistic or moral vision :

In the corrupted currents of this world
Offense's gilded hand may shove by justice,
And oft 'tis seen the wicked prize itself
Buys out the law: but 'tis not so above;
There is no shuffling, etc.

Again, we know that it is considered by many a beautiful, even a heroic, thing to tell a lie under stress of sentimental circumstances. Victor Hugo's Sister Simplice lied to save the fugitive, and has been blessed and applauded for the deed, just as Mr. Cable would have us bless and applaud Madame Del-

phine, who dies at the confessional
with the confession of a lie on her
lips. To Scott a higher grace was
revealed. As we stand by, in the
breathless court, listening with intent ears to catch the faintest whis-
per of a falsehood which the crowd,
the lawyers, the stern old father,
even the judge on the bench, and,
above all, the trembling sister at the
bar, are so eagerly expecting, but
which never passes the lips of
Jeanie Deans, we are thrilled with
the sublimity of true moral heroism.
Before the eyes of this honest Sir
Bors of fiction "the sweet Grail
glided and past," while others were
following "a mocking fire."

"Dr. Sevier" (1883), a beautiful
story told with the same exquisite
literary art and with even an added grace of simplicity, presents
the author with eyes toward the
setting sun; for his lack of ability
to construct a plot, and of power to
grasp the situation, is all too evident.

George W. Cable.

His canvas is so crowded with a multiplicity of details that it is impossible to obtain the right perspective, to give a true artistic grouping. The scene is laid in New Orleans, just prior to and including the Civil War. We catch a very imperfect glimpse of the more highly cultured society, and have an abundance of middle and low life; are taken into hospitals, foul jails with brutal keepers, along overflowed streets, through an epidemic of yellow fever; are made to witness the departure of troops from New Orleans and from New York, and carried through a series of most romantic and improbable adventures on the part of the heroine in passing through the lines of both armies; have to listen to a half-dozen dialects besides a lisping clergyman, witness the surrender of New Orleans, etc. In addition to the impossibility of handling so many details, the author's skill in narration at times deserts

George W. Cable.

him.   He " can devote ten pages to
an unsuccessful hunt for lodgings,
and a whole paragraph to a gesture."
The artist cannot be a suppresser of
truth, or an ignorer of facts, and the
omission of the negro, so curious
and marked that it must have been
of deliberate purpose, leaves a noticeable blank in the picture.   Was
it due to a slavery too dark and oppressive to be painted, or to the fear
of portraying the gentler aspects
and kindlier relations of master and
slave in a way which would seem
to soften and condone, that kept this
picturesque element out of the story
and prevented the author from giving the entire household of Dr. Sevier?   But the chief defect of the
book is the author's treatment of the
hero.   His trials and his difficulties
are real, true to life, though an in-
sufficient reason is assigned for them ;
for they were in a large measure the
author's own experiences.   Mr. Cable, however, did surmount his dif-

ficulties, because he had to contend
only with the fickle goddess, Fortune.
John Richling is at the mercy of the
caprice of the author. It is easy to
see that the poor fellow has no chance,
that the author intends first to make
him a failure, and then to kill him.
Why these useless efforts, this
hopeless suffering? Was it merely
that at the close of the story these
words might be put into the mouth
of the dying man? "'You know that
I am a native of Kentucky. My name
is not Richling. I belong to one of
the proudest, most distinguished families in that state or in all the land.
Until I married I never knew an
ungratified wish. I think my bringing up, not to be wicked, was as bad
as could be. It was based upon the
idea that I was always to be master,
and never servant. I was to go
through life with soft hands. I was
educated to know, but not to do.
When I left school my parents let
me travel. They would have let

335

me do anything except work. In
the West—in Milwaukee — I met
Mary. It was by mere chance. She
was poor, but cultivated and refined;
trained—you know—for knowing,
not doing. I loved her and courted
her, and she encouraged my suit,
under the idea, you know, again,'
he smiled fondly and softly—' that
it was nobody's business but ours.
I offered my hand and was accepted.
But when I came to announce our en-
gagement to my family, they warned
me that if I married her they would
disinherit and disown me.'

"'What was their reason, Richling?'

"'Nothing.'

"'But, Richling, they had a reason of some sort.'

"'Nothing in the world but that
Mary was a Northern girl. Simple
sectional prejudice. I didn't tell
Mary. I didn't think they would
do it; but I knew that Mary would
refuse to put me to the risk. We

married, and they carried out their threat.'

" The Doctor uttered a low exclamation, and both were silent."

As Richling seems to be one part of Mr. Cable, Dr. Sevier is another, now hard and repellant in his theories and then tenderly beautiful and poetic and loving in his life. If Richling had been developed into Dr. Sevier, a purpose would have been given to his life and a unity to the novel which would have insured to both the highest success. And the hand that drew Ristofalo with his quiet manner, happy disregard of fortune's caprices and real force of character, Narcisse—" dear, delicious, abominable Narcisse, more effective as a bit of coloring than all the Grandissimes put together "—and crowned him with the death of a hero, and gentle Mary bright, cheerful, brave, an ideal lover of her husband as he was of her, is certainly that of a master, as the imagination that con-

ceived them was that of a poet.
There are innumerable touches in
the story equal to anything that the
author has ever done—that is, as
beautiful as anything in contemporary fiction.

In 1879, upon the death of the
head of the commercial house in
which he was employed, Mr. Cable
formally entered upon a literary life.
He made his home far up in the
" garden district " of New Orleans
in a pretty cottage, painted in soft
tones of olive and red. A strip of
lawn bordered with flowers lay in
front of it, and two immense orange
trees, beautiful at all seasons of the
year, formed an arch above the steps
that led up to the piazza. The study,
where " The Grandissimes," " Madame Delphine," and " Dr. Sevier "
were written, was a room of many
doors and windows, with low book-
cases lining the walls, and adorned
with pictures in oil and water colors
by G. H. Clements, and in black and

338

white by Joseph Pennell. Mr. Cable has always carried his counting-room methods into his work, indexing and journaling his notes and references and so systematizing everything as to be able to turn to it without a moment's delay. He is untiring, and strives to be exact in his researches. "In making his notes," says Miss J. K. Wetherill, in "Authors at Home," "it is his usual custom to write in pencil on scraps of paper. These notes are next put into shape, still in pencil, and the third copy, intended for the press, is written in ink on note-paper—the chirography exceedingly neat, delicate, and legible."

Every one acquainted with old New Orleans has admired the accuracy, as well as the beauty, of his descriptions of houses, buildings, and places. As Mr. Lafcadio Hearn has remarked in the " Scenes of Cable's Romances "—a delightful article in the *Century* for November, 1883 :

George W. Cable.

" The sharp originality of Mr. Cable's descriptions should have con-
vinced the readers of 'Old Creole
Days' that the scenes of his stories
are in no sense fanciful; and the
strict perfection of his Creole architecture is readily recognized by all
who have resided in New Orleans.
Each one of those charming pictures
of places — veritable pastels — was
painted after some carefully selected
model of French or Franco-Spanish
origin—typifying fashions of build-
ing which prevailed in colonial days."
He is a rapid sketcher, taking in at
a glance almost every wrinkle on
the front of those old, quaint, picturesque buildings. His artistic temperament is most marked. " Music,
painting, and sculpture are full of
charms for him, and he is an intuitive judge of what is best in art.
His knowledge of music is far above
the ordinary, and he has made a
unique study of the usually elusive
and baffling strains of different song-

340

birds." After many efforts he succeeded in recording the roulade of
an oriole that used to sing in those
orange trees in front of his former
home. Of his family life in this
cottage Miss Wetherill has sketched
this beautiful picture: " Seemingly
sedate, Mr. Cable is full of fun ; and
charming as he is in general society,
a compliment may be paid him that
cannot often be spoken truthfully of
men of genius—namely, that he appears to the best advantage in his
own home. His children are a merry little band of five girls [now six]
and one boy, each evincing, young as
they are, some distinctive talent. It
is amusing to note their appreciation
of 'father's fun,' and his playful
speeches always give the signal for
bursts of laughter. This spirit of
humor, so potent to ' witch the heart
out of things evil,' is either hereditary or contagious, for all of these
little folks are ready of tongue. The
friends whom Mr. Cable left be-

hind him, in New Orleans, remember with regretful pleasure the delightful little receptions which have now become a thing of the past. Sometimes, at these gatherings, he would sing an old Scotch ballad, in his clear, sweet tenor voice, or one of those quaint Creole songs that he has since made famous on the lecture platform; or, again, he would read a selection from 'Dukesborough Tales,' one of his favorite humorous works. Nothing was stereotyped or conventional, for Mr. Cable is, in every aspect of life, a dangerous enemy to the commonplace." His reading throughout life, it would seem, has been thorough rather than general. For a long while he entertained scruples against novel - reading, but George MacDonald's "Annals of a Quiet Neighborhood" overcame his prejudice, and since then Victor Hugo, Thackeray, Tourguéneff, and Hawthorne have become his special favorites.

George W. Cable.

Mr. Cable's historical writings, " New Orleans before the Capture," " The Dance in Place Congo," two sketches, " New Orleans " in the census of 1880 and again in the Encyclopedia Britannica, and " The Creoles of Louisiana " (1884), are marked by the same clear, pictur- esque style and exquisite finish ob- servable in his romances. The facts have been collected with the most diligent research and painstaking labor, for the author was an earnest student of the French occupation of the Mississippi Valley before he was a writer of fiction. But though the memory is full, the horizon is not wide, and there need be no fear of canonization of either Creole or "American" so long as this skilful writer is both advocate and judge. A marvelous story, however—cov- ering nearly two hundred years, and telling of the origin of the peo- ple, the black code, the changes in ownership, the pirates at Barataria, the battle of New Orleans, the manners and characteristics of different generations of Creoles, epidemics, floods, and the wonderful growth of the Creole capital in spite of mishaps and disasters — is recounted with the simple directness and onward flow of an almost perfect narrative style. Dull or heavy topics are made inviting, and the picture of the commercial prosperity and importance of the Great South Gate "vies with fiction itself." When, however, the author essays to give "the derivation and final effect of influences," we become aware of the same spirit, too, which characterizes his imaginative productions. In truth this volume should be studied rather as the frame-work of the author's romances than as history; for it is to a large extent beautiful, picturesque, poetic-fiction. "Poetry," says the Autocrat in one of his inspired moments, "uses the rainbow

tints for special effects, but always
keeps its essential object in the purest white light of truth." For the
prejudiced observer this is an impossibility, since the real truth, the
secrets of life and of nature, are revealed only to loving, sympathetic
hearts. Now and then the author
does overcome his partisan feeling—
not against Creole or Southerner per
se, but always in relation to slavery—
sufficiently to write about the Creole
with real sympathy and genuine admiration : " By and by a cloud darkened the sky. Civil war came on.
The Creole in that struggle was little different from the Southerner at
large. A little more impetuous, it
may be ; a little more gaily reckless,
a little more prone to reason from
desire ; gallant, brave, enduring,
faithful ; son, grandson, great-grand-
son, of good soldiers, and a better
soldier every way and truer to himself than his courageous forefathers.
He was early at Pensacola. He

was at Charleston when the first
gun was fired. The first hero that
came back from the Virginia Penin-
sula on his shield was a Creole. It
was often he who broke the quiet
along the Potomac, now with song
and now with rifle-shot. He was
at Bull Run, at Shiloh, on all those
blood-steeped fields around Richmond. He marched and fought
with Stonewall Jackson. At Mobile, at the end, he was there. No
others were quite so good for siege-
guns and water-batteries. What
fields are not on his folded banners?
He went through it all. But we
will not follow him. Neither will
we write the history of his town in
those dread days. Arming, march-
ing, blockade, siege, surrender, military occupation, grass-grown streets,
hungry women, darkened homes,
broken hearts—let us not write the
chapter; at least, not yet."

In the summer of 1884 Mr. Cable left New Orleans, taking his

family first to Simsbury, Conn., and the following year establishing his home permanently at Northampton, Mass. Since that time his remarkable energy and force of character have found vent in various channels. He has become one of the most popular readers in America, and the discovery of the unusual faculty of interpretation which he possesses was one of those happy accidents in the lives of gifted men. It was while he was lecturing at Johns Hopkins University on the literary art, that he first read, upon the suggestion of President Gilman, some selections from his own writings. Receiving cordial appreciation, and realizing the possession of a rare gift, he at once and in his usual thorough manner set about disciplining it and making it most effective. It is announced that he will shortly repay some of the indebtedness of the New World to the Old, and give a

347

course of readings in Great Britain next fall. Shortly after settling in Northampton he resumed with new zeal the Bible studies which so greatly interested the boy-soldier by the camp-fire, and with a class of twelve he began a series of talks on the Sunday-school lessons, which very quickly yielded an enrollment of seven hundred. Later this work was transferred to Tremont Temple, Boston, where every Saturday afternoon for fifteen months he addressed twice that number. Contributions to the critical columns of the *Sunday-School Times*, under the title "A Layman's Hints" and "The Busy Man's Bible" (1891) grew out of these studies.

A still greater part of Mr. Cable's activity has been in connection with an investigation into the political and social status of the negro in the South. From many essays and addresses he has collected two small volumes, "The Silent South"

George W. Cable.

(1885), which also contains " The
Freedman's Case in Equity," and
" The Convict Lease System in the
Southern States," and " The Negro
Question " (1890).   In connection
with this work he organized the
" Open Letter Club," which was an
attempt to secure cooperation among
representative citizens of the South
for the scientific discussion of Southern problems ; but quickly realizing
how far apart he and they were,
he   dropped   it.   " Strange   True
Stories of Louisiana " (1888), a volume of romance from real life, belongs strictly to this period of controversy and is specially interesting
for the light that it throws on the
controversialist's methods. The two
most telling stories in the collection
are, " let it be plainly understood,"
not typical, but simply intended to
teach that " a public practice is an-
swerable for whatever can happen
easier with it than without it, no
matter whether it must, or only may,

349

happen." He has also edited "Creole Slave Songs" and a "West Indian Slave Insurrection."

It is no little relief to turn from this
perfervid political rhetoric to the
prose pastoral of "Bonaventure"
(1888), which, though not a great
novel, bids fair to outlive anything
that the author has yet written. It
consists of three stories, "Carancro,"
"Grand Pointe," and "Au Large,"
which appeared separately in the
Century. The opening scene takes
us at once

> among the few-acred farmers
> On the Acadian coast, and the prairies of
> fair Opelousas;

and the prospect which stretches
away, "fair and distant, in broad
level or gently undulating expanses
of crisp, compact turf, dotted at remote intervals by farms, each with
its low-roofed house, nestled in a
planted grove of oaks or, oftener,
pride of China trees," is typical of
the simple lives in the charming idyl.

George W. Cable.

The artist has hung a luminous atmosphere about them and touched them with heavenly colors of tenderest idealism, letting their lives, however, unfold themselves after a most realistic fashion. Bonaventure, with his noble simplicity, manly gentleness, and ardent enthusiasm, is perhaps the author's finest conception of character, though the characterization throughout is true to life. Bonaventure, Sidonie, Marguerite, Claude, St. Pierre, Mr. Tarbox, Madame Zosephine, are not delineations of character development, but actual lives lived before us ; and the atmosphere in which they live is as fresh and balmy and healthful as nature herself could produce in her rarest climes. It is a book to read not so much for the story as for the bewitching charm that comes from " some grace of expression, or ' cute ' touch of character, or exquisite description," to be found on every page.

George W. Cable.

In striking contrast with this charming volume is "John March Southerner" (1894)—one of the most dismal failures ever made by a man of genius. There is hardly a true note in it. An old Confederate soldier, plucky enough to fight to the end and brave enough to save the life of a comrade at the risk of his own, is chosen for the villain. He is called Rev. John Wesley Garnett, A.M., and made President of a college. He beats a negro unmercifully, slaps his grown daughter in the face, kills his wife with cruelty, swindles John March out of his estate, seduces his friend's wife, and then shoots the friend down on the street. The hero is " converted in a revival," but continues to carry his pistol and is ever ready to shoot. Jeff Jack, a secondary hero, is sent off on his "bridal tour" drunk; John March's mother is a silly, nervous, ridiculous Southern authoress. With the hero is contrasted a New

Englander, whose family is a model of domestic happiness, refinement, and culture, while he himself is endowed with gentleness, generosity, and almost every other grace and virtue. Legislative trickery, " booms," revengeful mountaineers, a negro politician, much incorrect dialect, and many other ingredients, are poured into this witch's caldron, where

Fair is foul and foul is fair.

The South can forgive Mr. Cable anything but literary failure. The " Taxidermist " and one or two other gems of recent years serve to show that the divine fire still burns. Would that it could be religiously consecrated to pure art!

Mr. Cable's New England home is a spacious house, with colonial buff walls and gambrel roofs, standing fair against the pines and chestnuts of Paradise Woods, on the edge of Northampton. It is situated on Dryad's Green, a short street, lead-

ing toward Mill River, made attractive by a line of narrow flower-beds
in the center, with the drives on
either side. The house is surrounded with spacious lawns and is only a
short distance from the woods, about
four acres of which Mr. Cable owns,
stretching from his home to the river. Woods is not the right word,
for it is rather a shady dell or woody
ravine, replete with bits of artistic
and rustic scenes, and little vistas,
simple yet full of beauty, kindle the
eye and gladden the heart. The dell
is completely shaded with a great
variety of noble trees, under which
small plants and trailing vines and
shrubbery are permitted to flourish.
From the terrace on which the house
stands a narrow ravine leads to the
river, and looking down this from
the terrace, through an opening
where the trees arch overhead, a view
of the river bend below can be obtained. The path into the woods is
fringed on either side with ferns,

wild rose and hazel wood. In these
" woods" Mr. Cable delights to
spend his moments of recreation,
with his intimate friends and companions—the birds, the wild flowers,
and the trees. Tree culture is his
hobby, and one of his fancies is to
adorn his grounds with trees trans-
planted by well-known men who
have from time to time been his
guests. The " Beecher elm," the
" Max O'Rell ash," the " Sol Smith
Russell linden tree," the " Felix
Adler hemlock," and the "A Co-
nan Doyle maple," all find hospitable entertainment on the lawn in
front of his house.

To the reading and lecture-going
public Mr. Cable's features are well
known; but no engraving or platform appearance gives the lurking
sparkle in the dark hazel eyes and
the peculiarly winning smile which
lights up the unusually bright and
intelligent face. In person Mr. Cable is small and slight, with chest-

nut hair, beard, and moustache, now somewhat silvered over; and there is a marked development of the forehead above the eyebrows. The full charm of an indescribable personality comes out in conversation, when a look, a shrug, or a bit of facial change gives a special seasoning to quaint turns of thought and felicitous phrases of expression. Since 1886 Mr. Cable has given much time to the Home Culture Clubs, which he organized on an original plan to carry light and health into individual lives and to bring different social elements together under the sympathetic influences of home life. Within the last month he has assumed the editorship of *Current Literature*, in which new field he will doubtless exercise a most helpful and stimulating influence upon the growth of literary taste and effort in America.

356

Charles Egbert Craddock.

THE appearance of Miss Mary
Noailles Murfree as a writer em-
phasized the fact that the old order of the South had utterly passed
away. For more than one hundred
years the different generations of
her family had been commonwealth-
builders, not writers. Her great-
great-grandfather, William Murfree,
was a member of the North Carolina Congress which met at Hali-
fax, November 12, 1776, for the purpose of framing a constitution for
the new state. A year before, his
son Hardy, just twenty-three years
old, had been made a captain in the
Continental line of his native state,
and at the capture of Stony Point
he had risen to the rank of major
and was in command of a body of
picked men. His descendants still
treasure the sash that he used in

helping to bear the mortally wounded Gen. Francis Nash from the battle-field of Germantown. Before independence was won, he was promoted again, and after peace reigned once more Col. Murfree "was found busy with his plantation" on the banks of Meherrin River, near Murfreesboro, N. C., till 1807, when he removed to Middle Tennessee, settling in Williamson County, on Murfree's fork of West Harpeth River. Those early settlers had an eye for rich lands and pleasant places. The town of Murfreesboro, not far off, was named in his honor, and his family throve and married well.

Just prior to the Civil War Hardy Murfree's grandson, William R. Murfree, was a successful lawyer in Nashville and the owner of a large amount of property in and about the city. His wife was Priscilla, the daughter of Mr. David Dickinson, whose residence, " Grantlands," near

Charles Egbert Craddock.

Murfreesboro, was in its day the most magnificent in that region. In this home was born, about 1850, a little girl to whom her parents gave the name Mary Noailles, but whom most people will prefer to remember as Charles Egbert Craddock.

In childhood a paralysis, which caused lameness for life, deprived her of all participation in the sports of children and set her bright and active mind to work to devise its own amusement and entertainment. Early sickness has more than once proved a blessing in disguise to the future writer of fiction by teaching him to train the observation, to live in good books, and to company with his fancies. It sent Scott to the country and to the fountains of legend and story, strongly inclined Dickens to reading, and laid Hawthorne upon the carpet to study the long day through. In the same way the Tennessee girl early developed a marked fondness for works of fic-

tion. It is easy to see that Scott and
George Eliot were her favorites, and
after reading with great earnestness
one of their stirring and enlarging
romances she would in her imagination body forth the entire story, in-
vesting mother, father, and other
members of the large household
with the characteristics of the persons of the powerful drama.

While an imagination originally
vivid was thus strengthened, her life
and surroundings encouraged a natural tendency to acute observation.
After the cordial Southern manner,
hospitality reigned in her home, and
the wide family connection and many
friends were equally hospitable. At
the academy in Nashville, where
she was put to school, she was associated with the daughters of the best
families in her own and neighboring
states. She must also have been
thrown much with her brother and
other boys, for few masculine writers show so thorough an under-

standing and appreciation of boy
nature. And then there were the
family servants, to whom every
Southern child of the old régime
was indebted for unique cultivation
of the fancy and many lasting impressions. To this day, it is said,
Charles Egbert C r a d d o c k finds
more enjoyment in a boy or darky
than in anything else.

This condition of society, along
with her father's and mother's large
estates, was swept away by the war.
The old Dickinson mansion was still
standing, and to this the family now
went, expecting to stay only a short
time, but remaining for years. This
is the house of " Where the Battle
Was Fought," and though the vivid
description of it and the battle-field
in the opening chapter of this novel
is somewhat fanciful, enough of the
reality remains to give us an accurate impression of the scenes amid
which she now lived.

" By wintry daylight the battle-

field is still more ghastly. Gray
with the pallid crab-grass which so
eagerly usurps the place of last summer's crops, it stretches out on every
side to meet the bending sky. The
armies that successively encamped
upon it did not leave a tree for miles,
but here and there thickets have
sprung up since the war, and bare
and black they intensify the gloom
of the landscape. The turf in these
segregated spots is never turned.
Beneath the branches are rows of
empty, yawning graves, where the
bodies of soldiers were temporarily
buried. Here, most often, their
spirits walk, and no hire can induce
the hardiest plowman to break the
ground. Thus the owner of the land
is fain to concede these acres to his
ghostly tenants, who pay no rent.
A great brick house, dismantled and
desolate, rises starkly above the dismantled desolation of the plain. Despite the tragic aspect of this build-
ing, it offers a certain grotesque sug-

gestion—it might seem in the mad ostentation of its proportions a vast caricature of succumbed prosperities. There is no embowering shrubbery about it, no enclosing fence. It is an integrant part of the surrounding ruin. Its cupola was riddled by a cannonade, and the remnants shake ominously with every gust of wind; there are black fissures in the stone steps and pavements where shells exploded; many of the windows are shattered and boarded up. . . . The whole place was grimly incongruous with the idea of a home, and as he [the hero of the story] was ushered into a wide, bare hall, with glimpses of uninhabited, unfurnished rooms on either hand, there was intimated something of those potent terrors with which it was instinct—the pursuing influences of certain grisly deeds of trust, for the battle-field, the gruesome thickets, the house itself, all were mortgaged."

As a recompense for this monoto-

nous and disheartening existence
amid scenes of former happiness
and splendor came the annual so-
journ of the family during the summer months in the mountains of
Eastern Tennessee, which was repeated for fifteen successive years.
Breathing this invigorating air, the
thoughtful girl also enjoyed the wild
birds and wilder flowers, the sylvan
glades and foaming cataracts, and
companioned daily with the Blue
Ridge, the Bald, the Chilhowee, and
the Great Smoky Mountains, whose
tops pierced the blue sky and whose
steep and savage slopes were covered
with vast ranges of primeval forest.
These scenes were so indelibly
etched upon her memory that in
after-years a rare profusion of
perfect pictures was easily obtainable. The very atmosphere itself
of her life at this period seems to
be preserved in the opening paragraph of "The Despot of Broom-
Sedge Cove:" "On a certain steep

and savage slope of the Great
Smoky Mountains the primeval
wilderness for many miles is unbroken save by one meager clear-
ing. The presence of humanity
upon the earth is further attested
only by a log cabin, high on the
rugged slant. At night the stars
seem hardly more aloof than the valley below. By day the mountains
assert their solemn vicinage, an aus-
tere company. The clouds that si-
lently commune with the great peaks,
the sinister and scathing deeds of the
lightnings, the passionate rhetoric of
the thunders, the triumphal pageant-
ry of the sunset tides, and the wist-
ful yearnings of the dawn aspiring
to day—these might seem the only
incidents of this lonely and exalted
life. So august is this mountain
scheme that it fills all the visible
world with its massive, multitudinous presence; still stretching into
the dim blue distances an infinite
perspective of peak and range and

lateral spur, till one may hardly believe that fancy does not juggle with
fact."

But the deepest interest of a nature rich in thought, imagination,
and wide human sympathy centered
in the dwellers among those wild and
rugged fastnesses. They were for
the most part descendants of the
earliest settlers in the Old North
State, and more than three-quarters
of a century before had climbed
over the high ranges which form a
natural boundary between Tennessee and her parent state and perched
on the mountain sides or nestled in
the coves of their new home. To
them the great world outside and
beyond the hazy boundaries of their
mountain ranges remained an un
known land; and the tide of modern progress dashed idly at the foot
of their primitive ideas and conserv-
ative barriers. There was no room
for progress, for the mountaineers
were not only satisfied with things

366

as they existed, but were unaware that there could be a different existence. For centuries no enlargement had come into their narrow individual lives and scant civilization, which to the casual observer seemed as bare and blasted as the "balds" upon the Great Smokies.

But to this acute and sympathetic observer were revealed not only the elemental qualities of our common humanity, but also the sturdy independence, integrity, strength of character, and finer feelings always found in the English race, however disguised by rugged exterior or hindered by harsh environment. Their honesty, their patriotism, their respect for law, their gloomy Calvinistic religion, their hospitality were in spite of the most curious modifications the salient points of a striking individuality and unique character. The mountains seemed to impart to them something of their own dignity, s o l e m n i t y and silence.

Charles Egbert Craddock.

Their archaic dialect and slow, drawl-ing speech could flash with dry hu-mor and homely mother-wit and glow with the white heat of biting sarcasm or lofty emotion. Their deliberate movements and impassive faces veiled deep feelings and pent-up passions, and they could be as sud-den and destructive as Nature her-self in her fiercer moods, or as ten-der and self-forgetful as Mary of Magdala. Fearless of man and open foes, the bravest of them shuddered at the mention of the " harnt of Thunderhead " and shrank from opening the graves of the "little people." Every stream and cave had its legend or spirit, and tower-ing crag and blue dome were chron-icled in tradition and story. No phase of this unique life escaped the keen eye and powerful imagination of the most robust of Southern wri-ters in this most impressible period of her life.

The growth of Craddock's art

can not now be traced with certainty, though it is known that she served an apprenticeship of nearly ten years before her stories began to make any stir in the world. The general belief, therefore, that her literary career began with the " Dancin' Party at Harrison's Cove," which appeared in the *Atlantic* for May, 1878, is incorrect. She used to contribute to the weekly edition of *Appleton's Journal*, which ceased publication in that form in 1876, and it is a little remarkable that her contributions were even then signed Charles E. Craddock. Two of her stories were left over, and one of them, published in "Appleton's Summer Book," in 1880, " Taking the Blue Ribbon at the Fair," rather indicates that she had not yet discovered wherein her true power lay. Although it is a pleasing little story, it is not specially remarkable for any of the finer qualities of her later writings ; and it appears out of place in a collection of stories published in 1895, as if it were a new production. The assumed name which her writings bore was finally determined upon by accident, though the matter had been much discussed in her family. It was adopted for the double purpose of cloaking failure and of securing the advantage which a man is supposed to have over a woman in literature. It veiled one of the best-concealed identities in literary history. More than one person divined George Eliot's secret, and the penetrating Dickens observed that she knew what was in the heart of woman. But neither internal nor external evidence offered any clue to Craddock's personality. The startlingly vigorous and robust style and the intimate knowledge of the mountain folk in their almost inaccessible homes, suggestive of the sturdy climber and bold adventurer, gave no hint of femininity, while certain portions of her writings, both in

370

thought and treatment, were peculiarly masculine.

In no way did Craddock betray "his" identity. Mr. Howells, who was the first to perceive the striking qualities of the stories, never suspected that the new writer was a woman ; and Mr. Aldrich, who shortly succeeded him, and one of whose first acts as editor was to write to " My Dear Craddock " for further contributions, was equally wide of the mark, though he mused considerably over the personality of the remarkably o r i g i n a l contributor. Once, indeed, he wrote asking how the latter could have become so intimate with the strange, quaint life of the mountaineers, but the pleasant reply threw no light upon the author's personality. Gradually, however, the mystery cleared away, though the final revelation was reserved for a particularly dramatic situation.

In the course of a year or two the editor and publishers learned that

Charles Egbert Craddock.

M. N. Murfree was the author's real name, and Mr. Aldrich rather prided himself, we are told, upon directing his communications thereafter to M. N. Murfree, Esq., feeling very confident that one who evinced such knowledge of the law as appeared in her writings and wrote with such a pen could be no other than a lawyer. The manuscript of " Mr." Craddock certainly had nothing feminine about it, with its large, bold characters, every letter as plain as print, and strikingly thick, black lines. So liberal indeed was the author in the use of ink that the editor had his little joke, as he was writing to ask for what proved to be the powerful novel of the " Prophet of the Great Smoky Mountains," remarking, " I wonder if Craddock has laid in his winter's ink yet, so that I can get a serial out of him." What was his surprise, therefore, as one Monday morning in March, 1885, he was called from the edito-

rial room, to find awaiting him below a young lady of slight form,
about five feet four inches in height,
with blond complexion and light-
brown, almost golden hair, bright,
rather sharp face, with all the features quite prominent—f o r e h e a d
square and projecting. eyes gray,
deep-set, and keen, nose Grecian,
chin projecting, and mouth large—
who quietly remarked that she was
Charles Egbert Craddock!

Miss Murfree's literary success
really began with the publication of
her collection of short stories, "In
the Tennessee Mountains," in May,
1884. It was at once recognized
that another Southern writer of un-
common art, originality, and power
had entered into a field altogether
new and perfectly fresh. Only here
and there was discernible the slightest trace of imitation in conception
or manner, while the atmosphere
was entirely her own; and to the
rare qualities of sincerity, simplicity,

and closeness of observation were added the more striking ones of vivid realization and picturing of scene and incident and character. Her magic wand revealed the poetry as well as the pathos in the hard, narrow, and monotonous life of the mountaineers, and touched crag and stream and wood and mountain range with an enduring splendor. All the admirable qualities of her art are present in this volume. The spontaneous, instinctive power of telling a story for its own sake proclaimed close kinship with Scott, while the exquisite word-painting and beautiful descriptions of mountain scenery, with all the shifting phases of spring and autumn, of sunset, mist, storm, and forest fire, could have been learned only in the school of Ruskin and of nature. In the profound and tragically serious view and contemplation of life she is the child of George Eliot and of the battle-scarred South. But her

374

real power, as is true of every writer that has been either an enriching
or an uplifting force in human lives,
rests upon a sympathetic understanding of human life. Her insight
into the o r d i n a r y, commonplace,
seemingly unpoetic lives of the
mountaineers, her tenderness for
them, her perception of the beauty
and the wonder of their narrow existence is one of the finest traits in
her character and her art. Through
this wonderful power of human
sympathy the delicately nurtured
and highly cultured lady entered
into the life of the common folk
and heard their heart-throbs under-
neath jeans and homespun. She
realized anew for her fellow men
that untutored souls are perplexed
with the same questions and shaken
by the same doubts that baffle the
learned, and that it is inherent in humanity to rise to the heroic heights
of self-forgetfulness and devotion to
duty in any environment. Indeed,

the key-note of her studies is found
in the last sentence of this volume:
" The grace of culture is, in its way,
a fine thing, but the best that art can
do—the polish of a gentleman—is
hardly equal to the best that nature
can do in her higher moods."

Each of these stories embodies a
"higher mood" of some uncultiva-
ted, simple soul influenced by a
noble motive, and the good lesson
taught with equal art and modesty
stirs the heart with refining pity and
admiration. Cynthia Ware's long
journeys on foot and heroic exer-
tions are rewarded with the pardon
of the unjustly imprisoned man
whom she loves, only to find that he
has never taken the trouble to ask
who secured his release, that his love
was but a little thing which he had
left in the mountains, and that while
she was waiting for him he was
married to some one else. Through
Craddock's skill we become witness-
es of this heart tragedy and enter

into the inner experience of a human soul which through suffering learns to adjust itself anew, "ceases to question and regret, and bravely does the work nearest her hand." Again it is the weak and slender Celia Shaw who painfully toils at night through the bleak, snow-covered woods to save the lives of the men whom her father and his friends had determined to "wipe out." Again and again in Craddock's writings the strange miracle of this sweet, trustful, loving, yet heroic girlhood appears amid the lonely, half-mournful life of the mountain folk, intensified by the attitude of the faded, gaunt, melancholy older women, "holding out wasted hands to the years as they pass—holding them out always and always empty"— with the grace, the beauty, and the pervasive fragrance of a wild rose in the wilderness. Our author seems to agree with George Eliot in thinking that "in these delicate vessels is

borne on through the ages the treasure of human affections."

Craddock's heroes — blacksmiths,
constables, herders, illiterate preachers, and other rude mountaineers—
are equally attractive in their way,
and are drawn with an even tenderer
and more skilful hand. She is a
master in depicting those situations
which touch the springs of pathos
or thrill the heart with a generous
elation. It does not matter whether
it is merely the noble impulse which
leads a Bud Wray, or in a later story
a Mink Lorey—" Mink by name
and Mink by nature "—to enthrone
in one supreme moment the better
part of his nature, or the settled purpose and lofty determination of a
Simon Burney, who gallantly de-
fends at the risk of his own life and
gives a permanent home to the ill-
tempered, worthless little " harnt "
that walks Chilhowee, saying with
noble simplicity : " I'll take keer of
ye agin them Grims ez long ez I kin

fire a rifle. An arter the jury hev
done let ye off, ye air welcome ter
live along o' me at my house till ye
die." The central idea or the strong
situation, however, is not unduly
stressed. The touches of incident
and of humor and the exquisite landscapes leave unfading impressions.
After thirteen years the ring of the
metaled hoof upon the flinty path
echoes in the memory, and the broad
antlers of the noble stag garlanded
with blossoming laurels stand out in
bold relief on the edge of the mountain road. One can still see the
highly imaginative picture of the
gamblers throwing their cards upon
the inverted basket, first by the light
of tallow dip and then by the blaze
of pine knots, while the moon shines
without and the hidden mimic of the
woods uncannily repeats their agitated tones. Nor is the reader likely
to forget the touch of grim humor
in the speech of the young mountaineer, glad that the "fightin' preach-

379

Charles Egbert Craddock.

er " had prevented him from killing
the outlaw and horse thief, yet naive-
ly remarking: "An' the bay filly
ain't sech a killin' matter, nohow;
ef it war the roan three-year-old,
now, 'twould be different."

The large and solemn presence of
Nature is never lost sight of, her various moods and manifestations being used, as a kind of chorus to in-
terpret the melancholy or the emotion of the human actors. The narrative is inlaid with exquisite bits of
landscape, serving not so much to
disclose the range and minuteness
of the author's observation—at least
in her earlier works—as to give expression to the fitting sentiment or
development to the appropriate passion. When the great beauty of the
style with which these fresh and robust stories were clothed is taken
into consideration, something of the
present pleasure and the richer anticipation of the readers of 1884 may
be imagined.

Charles Egbert Craddock.

In September, of the same year, "Where the Battle Was Fought" appeared, a story in which Craddock gives an effective picture of the devastation caused by the Civil War. The plot and the villains intriguing for a young girl's property are purely conventional, but so far from being a misstep this is a story of richest promise. The unmistakable bent of the author's genius is, it is true, shown in such creations as Toole, Graffy Beale, and Pickie Tait, while her superb landscape-painting has never been used more suggestively and impressively. "There is something Hawthornesque in the part which inanimate nature is made to play in this novel—a gigantic personification that wails and loves and hates—speechless, yet full of speech; tearless, yet fraught with innumerable tears; voiceless, yet full of tongues and languages." But the hand that sketched Marcia and General Vayne gave tokens of possibilities far greater than could be attained through Marcellys, Dorindas, Letitias, and Aletheas, or through prophets of the Great Smoky Mountains and despots of Broom-Sedge Cove, for Nature in her higher moods has never produced a Romola, a Portia, a Colonel Esmond, or a Sir Roger de Coverley. As the penetrating Sartor, in speaking of clothes, observes : " Nature is good, but she is not the best; here truly was the victory of Art over Nature." No one had a better chance to know the old Southern gentleman than Craddock, and that she had made use of her opportunity is more than suggested in her realistic description of General Vayne's moral magnifying-glass : " Through this unique lens life loomed up as rather a large affair. In the rickety court-house in the village of Chattalla, five miles out there to the south, General Vayne beheld a temple of justice. He translated an office-holder as the sworn servant of the people. The State was this great commonwealth, and its seal a proud escutcheon. A fall in cotton struck him as a blow to the commerce of the world. From an adverse political fortune he augured the swift ruin of the country. Abstract ideas were to him as potent elements in human affairs as acts of the Legislature, and in the midst of the general collapse his large ideals still retained their pristine proportions."

Such is the lifelike presentation of the sentiments of a certain type of old Southerner, and in the further portrayal of the one-armed ex-Confederate general the graphic touches of speech, manner, noble impulses, and actions are so true to nature that one readily recognizes the picture as a study from life. Though the story itself, however, does not present the orderly and artistic development and unfolding of a well-constructed plot, failing chiefly in coherence and a natural transition of scene and incident, and though it contains much that is undeniably conventional, yet its many strong and original features and powerful close leave the impression that this new departure contains the promise of richest possibilities which, it may be hoped, Craddock will some day realize for the world.

In her next volume, " Down the Ravine," our author takes us back to the mountains, and gives us a book for boys not easily matched in juvenile literature. Avoiding all sentimental weakness and set preachments, and conveying its fine and healthy moral in the whole spirit and atmosphere of the story, she unfolds plot and underplot simply, naturally, and with fine artistic effect. Scene, incident, and character are fused in the glow of a well-ordered imagination. The ubiquitous imp of a small boy is there, of course, but can the world do without him any better than the story-books?

and also the saving grace of a sister's quiet love and shaping influence, suggested with rare art and delicacy in little Tennessee's constant presence. But the crowning merit of the tale is the fresh and original presentation of the old story of a mother's love and the beauty of confidence between mother and son in a rude mountain home. "Don't everybody know a boy's mother air bound ter take his part agin all the worl'?" she asks with simple candor, and when misfortune touches him every trace of her caustic moods disappears and she becomes as gentle and tender and wise as if she had been nurtured in a lady's bower. Years afterward the son had not forgotten how stanchly she upheld him in every thought when all the circumstances belied him. 'Taint no differ ez long ez 'tain't the truth," said his mother, philosophically. "We-uns will jes' abide by the truth." "And day by day as he went to his work, meeting everywhere a short word or a slighting look, he felt that he could not have borne up, save for the knowledge of that loyal heart at home." This has all been told a thousand times, but never in a simpler, healthier, more natural way than in this delightful little volume. In unity of effect this is perhaps Craddock's most perfect story.

In the following October appeared "The Prophet of the Great Smoky Mountains," and almost every year since that time has witnessed the appearance of some new volume— "In the Clouds," 1886; "The Story of Keedon Bluffs," 1887; "The Despot of Broomsedge Cove," 1888; "In the Stranger Peoples' Country," 1891; "His Vanished Star," 1894; "The Phantoms of the Footbridge" and "The Mystery of the Witch-Face Mountain," 1895; while "The Jugglers," which has been running as a serial

Charles Egbert Craddock.

in the *Atlantic*, has just appeared,
and "The Mountain Boys" is announced for immediate publication.
Though the result is on the whole
disappointing—the rare promise of
the author's earlier work not being
fulfilled in her later more labored
efforts—Miss Murfree has taken a
place among the very best writers of
purely American fiction. The too
great regularity of production in
which she has indulged has led her
into dreary wastes of repetitious shal-
lows, and still more frequently has
weighted her stories with manner-
isms which mar the beauty and perfection of their art. The reader
soon begins to scent favorite epi-
thets and grandiloquent phrases, to
be on the lookout for the "gibbous"
moon, the "mellow" moon, the
"lucent, yellow" moon, and every
kind of moon that ever was and
never was, and to divine when the
katydid is to "twang a vibrant
note," or the night is to "sigh au-

dibly in sheer pensiveness," or the
song of the cicada is to be "charged
with somnolently melodious post-
meridian sentiment."

A still more serious complaint
may be urged against the author's
tendency to overdo landscape pictures, and to make needless digressions. Miss Murfree is, above all
things, a painter, and particularly in
her earlier works has given abundant evidence that she is a real artist
in adapting story and landscape to
each other. Her description, too,
serves a literary purpose, now expressing the fitting sentiment, anon
developing the appropriate passion.
She seizes and interprets physical
features and natural phenomena in
their relation to various aspects of
human life with at times unerring
precision, vigor, and dramatic force.
Indeed, the scenery of the mountains is essential to the comprehen-
sion of the gloom of the religion,
the sternness of the life, the un-

couthness of the dialect, and the harshness of the characters presented in her stories.

All her digressions are not irrelevant. Oftentimes what seems to be a mere digression is according to nature, and used with significant effect in the presentation of mountain scene, life, and character. The result is a complete and perfect picture. The mountaineers are proverbially slow of speech and of thought, and during their long reflective pauses in conversation the skilful narrator must interest the mind of the reader just as in real life the listener would seek something for his mind to dwell upon. This gives lifelikeness to the picture, and, like a sweet interlude in music, a charming bit of description serves to fill in delightfully the intervening moments which would otherwise seem unreasonably long and tedious. The opening pages of " The Despot of Broomsedge Cove" reveal the author at work in her happiest vein and making the best use of this extraordinary gift. With a few skilful touches the corn-field, the winding road, the three mountaineers, each with his salient features of look, gait, and character, made known in the fewest possible words, and the glorious mountain view, are made to stand out before us as in real life, so that the reader becomes identified with the story and naturally shares in the conversation.

"'The Sperit has been with me strong, mighty strong, ter-day,' said Teck Jepson suddenly. 'I hev been studyin' on Moses, from the time he lef' the saidges by the ruver-bank,' he added, bridling with a sentiment that was strikingly like the pride of earth. Then as he gazed down at the landscape his face softened and grew pensive." "The great ranges were slowly empurpled against the pale eastern horizon, delicately blue, for the sun was in the western skies. How splendidly saffron those vast spaces glowed! What purity and richness of tint! Here and there were pearly wing-like sweeps of an incomparable glister; and the clouds, ambitious, must needs climb the zenith, with piled and stately mountainous effects, gleaming white, opaque, dazzling. The focal fires of the great orb were unquenched, and still the yellow, divergent rays streamed forth; yet in its heart was suggested that vermilion smoldering of the sunset, and the western hills were waiting."

" ' 'Twas tur'ble hard on Moses,' said Teck Jepson, ' when the Lord shut him out'n Canaan, arter travelin' through the wilderness. Tur'-ble hard, tur'ble hard!'" During another pause the reader learns that this slow talker has an imagination aflame with the trials of Moses, the glories of Solomon, the atrocities of

Charles Egbert Craddock.

Ahab and Jezebel; and in his igno-
rance it had never occurred to him
that his Biblical heroes had lived
elsewhere than in the Great Smoky
Mountains. "Their history had to
him an intimate personal relation, as
of the story of an ancestor in the
homestead ways and closely familiar.
He brooded upon these narrations,
instinct with dramatic movement,
enriched with poetic color, and lo-
calized in his robust imagination,
till he could trace Hagar's wild
wanderings in the fastnesses; could
show where Jacob slept and piled
his altar of stones; could distinguish
the bush, of all others on the ' bald,'
that blazed with fire from heaven,
when the angel of the Lord stood
within it." In every way this is a
model introductory chapter, and
every incident, bit of description,
explanatory digression, and situation serves as an admirable background for the heroic picture of
the Despot, whose impressive per-

sonality, in spite of qualities that would naturally inspire aversion, compels our admiration.

But far too often in her later stories the author's descriptions of natural scenery and observations of natural phenomena are excessive. In this paticular novel they reach the point of downright padding. The pictures are exceedingly well done, and the observations are sometimes very acute and perfectly true; but they are altogether out of place, and serve only to interrupt the action and to make the reader chafe, till he learns to skip. As a specimen of this provoking method we may take the account of Parson Donnard's endeavor to find out whether it is a " human critter " or the devil himself that lights the nightly fires of the lonely forge. He and his hypocritical scamp of a son are sitting on a rock in the dead of the night with every nerve a-quiver; momently we are expecting a solution of the mystery, but instead of this we are kept waiting with remarks about the stars, the darkness, the stony passes, the briers. Then we have shooting-stars and the clarion cock, and then again while the ignorant and superstitious old mountain preacher is intent upon his hand-to-hand grapple with the archfiend the author credits him with this series of sophisticated observations : "He noted how he seemed to face the great concave of the sky, how definite the western mountains stood against the starry expanse, how distinct certain objects had become even in the pitchy blackness, now that his eyes were in some sort accustomed to it."

It may readily be acknowledged that Miss Murfree's people are the people of the district she describes. Folk and mountains belong together. But she deals with life rather as a whole, as a community, a class, at best as a type. She has not succeeded in creating any indi-

Charles Egbert Craddock.

vidual or distinct character. Even
Cynthia Ware, Dorinda Cayce, Al-
ethea Sayles, Letitia Pettingill, and
Marcelly Strobe, the heroines in as
many different stories, are but va-
riants of one and the same type.
Slight changes are introduced in
adapting them to different situations,
but the characters all seem to be
drawn from the same model. A
graver defect is noticeable in the
author's treatment of her heroes, wherein she shows a fatal
inability to sustain character. When
the Prophet is introduced, revealing
in the quick glance of his eye
" fire, inspiration, frenzy—who can
say? " the reader is thrilled at the
prospect of a masterly delineation.
He expects to travel along the
narrow border-land between spiritual exaltation and insanity. But
in only one of Miss Murfree's
stories, " The Dancin' Party at
Harrison's Cove," does she reveal
a sympathetic understanding and

395

appreciation of the character of the minister. With the circuit-riders and pa'sons she seems to have had no personal acquaintance. They are drawn just as we would expect them to be depicted by one whose sole information was based on tradition, hearsay, and imagination. Nor does Craddock at any time exhibit that profound knowledge of the human heart and sympathetic insight into spiritual matters revealed by George Eliot in the character of Dinah Morris. Pa'son Kelsey remains hazy and indistinct throughout the story, the reader is left in doubt as to his sanity, and the catastrophe throws little light upon his character.

The Despot offered even a greater opportunity for masterly portraiture. In conception this is one of the most original and striking figures to be found in contemporary literature. This dauntless rider, singing his ecstatic psalms, this arrogant inter-

Charles Egbert Craddock.

preter of "the Lord's will," this
firm believer in his own might and
goodness, captivates the imagination of the reader from the first moment of his dramatic introduction :
"A moment more and the young
psalmist came around a curve, gal-
loping recklessly along beneath the
fringed boughs of the firs and the
pines, still singing aloud; the reins
upon his horse's neck, his rifle held
across the pommel of the saddle;
his broad hat thrust upon the back
of his head, his eyes scarcely turning toward the men who stood by
the wayside. . . . The rider
drew rein. The rapt expression of
his countenance abruptly changed.
He fixed imperative, worldly eyes
upon the speaker. They were deeply set, of a dark blue color, full of
a play of expression, and, despite
the mundane intimations of the moment, they held the only suggestions in his face of a spiritual possibility. He had a heavy lower

jaw, stern and insistent. A firm,
immobile mouth disclosed strong,
even teeth. His nose was slightly
aquiline, and he had definitely
marked black eyebrows. . . .
There was a strong individuality,
magnetism, about him, and before
his glance the peremptory spirit of
his interlocutor was slightly abated."

After a few chapters, however,
the author seems to lose interest in
the working out of her original conception. The hero is discarded for
other matters, while at the same
time the author's grip of the narrative suffers loss, and the way is
paved for irrelevant landscapes and
digressions. Even the hero's connection with the tragedy of the
story is accidental, and the heroine
gradually absorbs the interest and
the attention of the reader. The
author almost invariably leaves her
chief characters looking sadly, if
not hopelessly, into the future.

Perhaps Miss Murfree has at-

Charles Egbert Craddock.

tempted an impossible task in seek-
ing to invest the meager life and
primitive character of the mountaineers with an annual interest. When
the author of " Jane Eyre"—a novel
whose phenomenal success would
have greatly enhanced the value of
any work from her pen—was im-
portuned to write a new story, she
quietly answered : " I have told all
I knew in the last one, and I must
wait two or three years, till I learn
something more, before I can write
again."

But the sweep and power of Miss
Murfree's narrative in all her finer
stories is sufficient to carry the reader over greater difficulties than these.
Story-telling is her true vocation.
She is no essayist or historian drawn
by the fashion of the time into the
facile fields of fiction. Fresh material and picturesque character lend,
it is true, their unique charms ; but,
after all, we are interested in this
writer chiefly on account of the

399

Charles Egbert Craddock.

stories she has to tell of the lives of
men and women whose traits are in
common with those of all times and
all places. While, however, the
reader's desire is to reach the end of
any of her stories and " see how it
comes out," still there are many
places where he delights to linger.
There are whole chapters in which
scene, situation, and incident are
handled without a flaw. The
situations are admirably planned,
the incidents inimitably related.
The author can be descriptive or
dramatic at will, and shows the
command of a humor which has the
tang but not the deep thought and
mellow wisdom of George Eliot's.

In the meeting between Teck
Jepson and Marcelly we lose sight
of the author, so completely does
she identify herself with the characters. We feel the fascination of
this girl as she sits upon the ledge
of a rock, and delight in the picture
of the old dog lying wheezingly

400

down in the folds of her blue
dress, " closing his eyes in a sort of
blinking resignation " at the rain-
storm, or rising to yawn, " stretching himself to his extreme length,
rasping his long claws on the
stones," and so rousing the Despot's impatience that he bids the
hound " hush up ! " Her stories
abound in these graphic scenes.
Nor would it be true to life if the
humor were left out. Chaucer,
Shakespeare, Scott, George Eliot,
Lowell, Joel Chandler Harris, Ian
Maclaren—all English writers who
excel in depicting the life and character of the common people—make
prominent their wit and humor. It
is a characteristic of the race. The
Tennessee mountaineer is noted for
his dry, caustic speech, and under
his slow drawl and rustic manners
are concealed no little practical wisdom and shrewd observation. Of
course geniality and playful fancy
do not flourish in so harsh a region,

but there is no lack of pungent, pithy sayings. This humor pervades the mountains. " Wall, 'pears like to me," says the filly-like Mirandy Jane, " ez Brother Jake Tobin sets mo' store on chicken fixin's than on grace, an' he fattens ev'y year." Old Mis' Cayce quaintly remarks : " I 'member when I war a gal whisky war so cheap that up to the store at the settlemint they'd hev a bucket set full o' whisky an' a gourd, free fur all comers, an' another bucket alongside with water ter season it. An' the way that thar water lasted war surprisin'; that it war ! " The dull old constable declares that " sech spellin' as Clem Sanders kin do oughter be agin the law ! It air agin every law o' spellin'. Clem ought to be hung a leetle fur each offense. It jes' fixes him in his criminal conduct agin the alphabet." Dorinda Cayce, when the sheriff, who has just enjoyed her mother's good dinner, ac-

Charles Egbert Craddock.

cuses her of harboring a fugitive,
quietly remarks : " 'Pears like ter
me ez we gin aid an' comfort ter
the officer o' the law ez well ez we
could." Letitia Pettingill's bright
sayings lighten up many a page
of " In the Stranger Peoples' Country," as well as the lot of the seemingly deserted wife ; and Marcelly's
imperative old grandmother makes
the doctor, and many another, writhe
under the hail of her stinging sarcasm. Without this pungent humor the distinct flavor of the inner
life of the strange, unique inhabitants of the mountains would be
lost.

Here, then, we have originality,
robust vigor, womanly insight, and
the charm of a born story-teller
brought to bear with genuine art
upon a fresh field and a unique civilization. Much of her later work
may have suffered from an attach-
ment to the narrow sphere of the
mountain folk ; but such are her

403

strength of purpose and great capa-
bility that it is not unreasonable yet
to expect the complete fulfilment of
the promise of her earlier work, if
the larger world may demand a
share of her attention and energies.

INDEX